P9-DFB-970

COMPREHENSIVE RESEARCH
AND STUDY GUIDE

Shakespeare's Sonnets and Poems

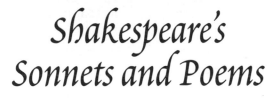

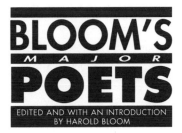

EDITED AND WITH AN INTRODUCTION
BY HAROLD BLOOM

BLOOM'S MAJOR DRAMATISTS

Anton Chekhov
Henrik Ibsen
Arthur Miller
Eugene O'Neill
Shakespeare's Comedies
Shakespeare's Histories
Shakespeare's Romances
Shakespeare's Tragedies
George Bernard Shaw
Tennessee Williams

BLOOM'S MAJOR NOVELISTS

Jane Austen
The Brontës
Willa Cather
Charles Dickens
William Faulkner
F. Scott Fitzgerald
Nathaniel Hawthorne
Ernest Hemingway
Toni Morrison
John Steinbeck
Mark Twain
Alice Walker

BLOOM'S MAJOR SHORT STORY WRITERS

William Faulkner
F. Scott Fitzgerald
Ernest Hemingway
O. Henry
James Joyce
Herman Melville
Flannery O'Connor
Edgar Allan Poe
J. D. Salinger
John Steinbeck
Mark Twain
Eudora Welty

BLOOM'S MAJOR WORLD POETS

Geoffrey Chaucer
Emily Dickinson
John Donne
T. S. Eliot
Robert Frost
Langston Hughes
John Milton
Edgar Allan Poe
Shakespeare's Poems & Sonnets
Alfred, Lord Tennyson
Walt Whitman
William Wordsworth

BLOOM'S NOTES

The Adventures of Huckleberry Finn
Aeneid
The Age of Innocence
Animal Farm
The Autobiography of Malcolm X
The Awakening
Beloved
Beowulf
Billy Budd, Benito Cereno, & Bartleby the Scrivener
Brave New World
The Catcher in the Rye
Crime and Punishment
The Crucible

Death of a Salesman
A Farewell to Arms
Frankenstein
The Grapes of Wrath
Great Expectations
The Great Gatsby
Gulliver's Travels
Hamlet
Heart of Darkness & The Secret Sharer
Henry IV, Part One
I Know Why the Caged Bird Sings
Iliad
Inferno
Invisible Man
Jane Eyre
Julius Caesar

King Lear
Lord of the Flies
Macbeth
A Midsummer Night's Dream
Moby-Dick
Native Son
Nineteen Eighty-Four
Odyssey
Oedipus Plays
Of Mice and Men
The Old Man and the Sea
Othello
Paradise Lost
A Portrait of the Artist as a Young Man
The Portrait of a Lady

Pride and Prejudice
The Red Badge of Courage
Romeo and Juliet
The Scarlet Letter
Silas Marner
The Sound and the Fury
The Sun Also Rises
A Tale of Two Cities
Tess of the D'Urbervilles
Their Eyes Were Watching God
To Kill a Mockingbird
Uncle Tom's Cabin
Wuthering Heights

COMPREHENSIVE RESEARCH
AND STUDY GUIDE

Shakespeare's Sonnets and Poems

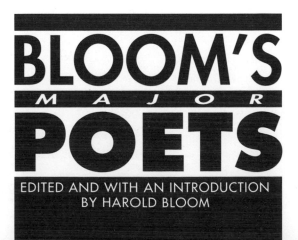

BLOOM'S
MAJOR
POETS

EDITED AND WITH AN INTRODUCTION
BY HAROLD BLOOM

© 1999 by Chelsea House Publishers, a division of Main Line Book Co.

Introduction © 1999 by Harold Bloom

3 5 7 9 8 6 4 2

Chelsea House Publishers
1974 Sproul Road, Suite 400
Broomall, PA 19008-0914

Library of Congress Cataloging-in-Publication Data

Shakespeare, William, 1564–1616.
[Selections.   1998]
Shakespeare's sonnets and poems / edited and with an introduction
by Harold Bloom.
p.   cm.—(Bloom's major poets)
Includes bibliographical references and index.
ISBN 0-7910-5107-2 (hc)
1. Sonnets, English.   I. Bloom, Harold.   II. Title.   III. Series.
PR2842.B58   1998
821'.3—dc21
98-31661
CIP

Contributing Editor: Mirjana Kalezic

Contents

User's Guide   7

Editor's Note   8

Introduction   9

Biography of William Shakespeare   13

Analysis of Shakespeare's Sonnets   15

Critical Views on Sonnet 19:

    Joseph Pequigney on The Poet's Relationship with Time   19

    Joel Fineman on Poetry and Progeny in the Sonnets   21

    Helen Vendler on the Altered Nature of Time in Sonnet 19   23

Critical Views on Sonnet 53:

    Hilton Landry on Platonism's Influence in Sonnet 53   25

    Murray Krieger on the Friend as Both One and Many in the Sonnets   27

    Stephen Booth on the Role of Paradox in Sonnet 53   28

    Joseph Pequigney on the Case Against Platonism in Sonnet 53   30

    Jonathan Bate on Shakespeare's Innovation in Sonnet 53   32

Critical Views on Sonnet 55:

    G. Wilson Knight on Sonnet 55 and the Power of Poetry   33

    Lowry Nelson Jr. on Rhyme in the Sonnets   34

    Howard Felperin on Shakespeare's Rhetorical Strategy in Sonnet 55   35

    Anthony Hecht on the Classical Roots of Sonnet 55   37

Critical Views on Sonnet 87:

    Murray Krieger on the Poet's Punctured Dream   39

    Joseph Pequigney on the Role of Physical Passion in Sonnet 87   41

    Jonathan Bate on Reading Beyond the Text of Sonnet 87   42

    Anthony Hecht on the Question of Blame in Sonnet 87   43

    Harold Bloom on the Meaning of "Misprision" in Sonnet 87   44

Critical Views on Sonnet 94:

    Sir William Empson on the Use of Flattery in Sonnet 94   45

    Edward Hubler on the Familiar Imagery in Sonnet 94   47

    Northrop Frye on the Youth's Inability to Produce Love   49

    Stephen Booth on Sonnet 94 and Readers' Expectations   49

    Harold Bloom on Sonnet 94 as a Forerunner to Shakespeare's Tragedies   52

    Helen Vendler on Shakespeare's Use of Plant Metaphors in Sonnet 94   54

Critical Views on Sonnet 116

  Murray Krieger on Poetry as a Testament to Immortality 55

  Richard Lanham on Rhetoric and the Truth of Love in
    Sonnet 116 57

  Stephen Booth on Substance and Emptiness in Sonnet 116 58

  Lowry Nelson Jr. on the Strength of Shakespeare's Rhyme
    in Sonnet 116 60

  Joseph Pequigney on the Poet's Love for the Youth Versus His
    Lust for the Mistress 61

  Helen Vendler on Sonnet 116 as a Rebuttal 62

Critical Views on Sonnet 129

  Richard Levin on the Evolution of Emotion in Sonnet 129 65

  Thomas M. Greene on "The Expence of Spirit" and Social Class 69

  Joel Fineman on the Paradox of Praise in the Dark Lady Sonnets 70

Summary Analysis of "The Phoenix and Turtle" 72

Critical Views on "The Phoenix and Turtle"

  Ronald Bates on Past Critical Errors in Analyzing the Poem 73

  G. Wilson Knight on the Birds' Respective Genders 74

  Murray Copland on the Poem and Platonism 76

Summary Analysis of The Rape of Lucrece 79

Critical Views on The Rape of Lucrece:

  Richard Lanham on the Importance of Language over
    Passion in the Poem 82

  Katharine Eisaman Maus on Language and Accountability
    in the Poem 84

  Heather Dubrow on the Poem's Rhetorical Ambiguities 86

Summary Analysis of Venus and Adonis 90

Critical Views on Venus and Adonis

  Jonathan Bate on Shakespeare's Rhetoric of Desire 93

  Richard Lanham on the Narrator's Detachment 94

  Nancy Lindheim on Vulnerability and Powerlessness in the Poem 96

  Heather Dubrow on How the Poet Shapes Our Responses 99

  John Klause on Why Venus and Adonis Can Be Redeemed 100

  Tita French Baumlin on Shakespeare and His Predecessors 102

  Jonathan Bate on Ovid's Influence on Shakespeare 104

Works by William Shakespeare 105

Works about Shakespeare's Sonnets and Poems 107

Index of Themes and Ideas 110

User's Guide

This volume is designed to present biographical, critical, and bibliographical information on the author's best-known or most important poems. Following Harold Bloom's editor's note and introduction are a detailed biography of the author, discussing major life events and important literary accomplishments. A thematic and structural analysis of each poem follows, tracing significant themes, patterns, and motifs in the work.

A selection of critical extracts, derived from previously published material from leading critics, analyzes aspects of each poem. The extracts consist of statements from the author, if available, early reviews of the work, and later evaluations up to the present. A bibliography of the author's writings (including a complete list of all books written, cowritten, edited, and translated), a list of additional books and articles on the author and the work, and an index of themes and ideas in the author's writings conclude the volume.

$\sim$

Harold Bloom is Sterling Professor of the Humanities at Yale University and Henry W. and Albert A. Berg Professor of English at the New York University Graduate School. He is the author of over 20 books and the editor of more than 30 anthologies of literary criticism.

Professor Bloom's works include *Shelley's Mythmaking* (1959), *The Visionary Company* (1961), *Blake's Apocalypse* (1963), *Yeats* (1970), *A Map of Misreading* (1975), *Kabbalah and Criticism* (1975), and *Agon: Toward a Theory of Revisionism* (1982). *The Anxiety of Influence* (1973) sets forth Professor Bloom's provocative theory of the literary relationships between the great writers and their predecessors. His most recent books include *The American Religion* (1992), *The Western Canon* (1994), *Omens of Millennium: The Gnosis of Angels, Dreams, and Resurrection* (1996), and *Shakespeare: The Invention of the Human*, 1998.

Professor Bloom earned his Ph.D. from Yale University in 1955 and has served on the Yale faculty since then. He is a 1985 MacArthur Foundation Award recipient and served as the Charles Eliot Norton Professor of Poetry at Harvard University in 1987–88. He is currently the editor of other Chelsea House series in literary criticism, including BLOOM'S NOTES, BLOOM'S MAJOR SHORT STORY WRITERS, MAJOR LITERARY CHARACTERS, MODERN CRITICAL VIEWS, MODERN CRITICAL INTERPRETATIONS, and WOMEN WRITERS OF ENGLISH AND THEIR WORKS.

Editor's Note

As there are forty-five Critical Views briefly extracted in this volume, I will indicate only a handful or so of what I take to be some of the high points among them. My Introduction broods on high irony in the Sonnets, and on the enigma of what I judge to be the augmenting rancidity of Shakespeare's vision of sexuality in his later plays.

Critical Views range from the inspired formalism of Helen Vendler through the careful old historicism of Stephen Booth and, in a very different mode, the vatic thematicism of George Wilson Knight. The new historicism of Joel Fineman, the influence-study of Jonathan Bate, and the feminism of Heather Dubrow help to complete the panoply of critical approaches, as do the historicized rhetorical studies of Richard Lanham. The evident homoeroticism of the Sonnets is examined by Joseph Pequigney, while Thomas Greene exemplifies a rare scholarly survival of Renaissance Humanist concerns. The archetypalism of Northrop Frye and the poetic authority of Anthony Hecht add further dimensions to this large theater of Shakespearean commentary.

Introduction

HAROLD BLOOM

It is a wholly truthful critical commonplace to assert that the strongest of Shakespeare's Sonnets and his "The Phoenix and Turtle" are among the best shorter poems in the English language. Since this volume reprints part of what I have written elsewhere on Sonnets 87 and 94, I confine this Introduction to 19, 53, 55, 116, and 129, as well as to "The Phoenix and Turtle."

Astonishing as the Sonnets remain, they are of a different order than, say, *As You Like It, Henry IV, 1 and 2, Hamlet, Twelfth Night, Measure for Measure, King Lear, Macbeth, Antony and Cleopatra, The Winter's Tale,* and about a dozen other Shakespearean dramas. Most simply, the Sonnets do not invent (or, if you prefer, represent) human beings. Necessarily more lyric than dramatic, these poems have their clear affinities with Falstaff and Hamlet, and many more of Shakespeare's protagonists, and yet the affinities remain enigmatic. Unless you are a formalist or an historicist, then Falstaff and Hamlet will compel you to see them as larger even than their plays, and as more "real" than actual personages, alive or dead. But the speaker of the Sonnets presents himself as a bewildering series of ambiguities. He is not and yet he is William Shakespeare the playmaker, and his two loves of comfort and despair, a young nobleman and a dark woman, never have the substance or persuasive force of Antony and Cleopatra, and of their peers in the greater plays. Shakespearean characters are adventures in consciousness; even the speaker of the Sonnets evades that immensity. Of the inwardness of the fair young man and of the dark lady, we are given only intimations.

We cannot recover either the circumstances or the personal motives (if any) of the Sonnets. *Love's Labour's Lost,* uniquely among the plays, partly shares the language of the Sonnets. Shakespeare's apparent dilemma in the Sonnets, rejection by beloved social superior, seems analogous to Falstaff's predicament in the *Henry IV* plays, but the speaker of the Sonnets has little of Sir John Falstaff's vitality, wiliness, and aplomb. Some of the Sonnets turn violently aside from life's lusts and ambitions, but these revulsions only rarely are rendered in Hamlet's idiom. It is dangerous to seek illuminations for the plays in the Sonnets, though sometimes you can work back from the dramatic to the lyric Shakespeare. The poetic achievement of the Sonnets has just enough of the playwright's uncanny power to show that we confront the same writer, but the awesome cognitive originality and psychological persuasiveness of the major dramas are subdued in all but a few of the sequences.

Formalist analysis of the Sonnets has been lifted to the apotheosis by Helen H. Vendler, just as contextual exegesis was perfected by Stephen Booth. As I am neither a formalist nor an historicist, old or new, nor a feminist, Marxist, mock-Parisian critic, I go at the Sonnets my own way, gleaning traces of Shakespeare's invention of the human, which is the grandest glory of his plays. The fair youth (presumably Southampton) and the dark lady are shadows, while the rival poet (probably Marlowe) is less than that. Only one human is invented in the Sonnets, and he is not quite a represenation of Shakespeare himself. "Selfsame" with Shakespeare he is not, yet he lingers near Shakespeare, and fascinates us by that proximity.

The funniest observation I know concerning Shakespeare's own sexual stance in regard to the Sonnets is Stephen Booth's:

"Homosexuality: William Shakespeare was almost certainly homosexual, bisexual, or heterosexual. The sonnets provide no evidence on the matter."

Taking the Sonnets together with the plays, Booth's contention seems a touch too formalist. One does not know, and one isn't going to know, but it seems not improbable that Shakespeare was bisexual, at least during certain periods of his life. The erotic, which crosses the sexual with the shadow of death, is in any case a larger category than any actual sexual experience. "Evidence" is also hardly the issue, unless you are Senator Trent Lott and the Christian Coalition, who would presumably wish to excise Shakespeare from our national culture, should the Bard's bisexuality be proved. Walt Whitman is our national poet, but he must be discarded also, in company with so many of the best poets of our last century. George Wilson Knight, one of my mentors in criticism, remarked to me, back in the mid-fifties, that only the blindly bigoted could fail to recognize homoerotic passion throughout Shakespeare, the Sonnets included. Wilson Knight was a fiercely thematic critic, but also an experiential one, and whether or not Shakespeare actually was the Earl of Southampton's physical lover (and the lover of other men, as well), the erotic intensity of Sonnets 1–126 does seem to me indisputable. Still, the erotic anguish is vastly augmented from 127 on, when the fatal Dark Lady enters the sequence. Gently pointing this out to Wilson Knight, I inspired him to the reflection that Platonic love was necessarily of a higher and more ideal order than I could understand. This indeed may be, though it would be difficult to decide whether the Speaker of the Sonnets suffers more deeply before or after 127. Certainly the modes of suffering are very different; before 127, the speaker's sorrows have a wonderful detachment to them. From 127 on, he lives (if that is the right word) inside a furnace.

From at least *Measure for Measure* and *Othello*, on through *The Two Noble Kinsmen*, sexuality is represented primarily as a torment—sometimes comic, more often not. As an archaic Bardolator, I am not inclined to separate this dramatic version of human reality from the playwright himself. Formalist and historicist critics frequently give me the impression that they might be more at home with Flaubert than with Shakespeare. The high erotic rancidity of *Troilus and Cressida, All's Well that Ends Well,* and *Timon of Athens* is too consistently ferocious to be dramatic artifice alone, at least in my experience as a critical reader. The bed-trick, harlotry, and venereal infection move very near the center of Shakespeare's vision of sexuality.

2.

Only a few of the Sonnets open as powerfully as 19: "Devouring Time, blunt thou the lion's paw." This line indeed is too powerful for a poem that concludes: "my love shall in my verse ever live young." Even had Southampton (or whoever) been the most beautiful youth in Elizabethan England, the diminishment would be considerable, except for the subtly implied irony that equates burning "the long-lived phoenix in her blood" with the first wrinkle that might appear on the young man's brow. The phoenix uniquely will be resurrected from time's flame; that brow will not, except in Shakespeare's sonnets. Any comfort involved would seem to belong to the poet, and not to his patron.

An even subtler irony prevails in Sonnet 53, where the magnificent opening question is beyond answer:

> What is your substance, whereof you are made,
> That millions of strange shadows on you tend?

Such a being is not going to manifest the "constant heart," which wistfully ends the poem. The sonnet's speaker—let us call him Shakespeare—is hardly deceived, or even deceivable, and clearly he anticipates rejection. He also anticipates literary immortality, which makes me doubt our legends of a careless Shakespeare, whose Sonnets were pirated, and whose plays were purely commercial enterprises.

"Not marble nor the gilded monuments," Sonnet 55, again asserts the beloved's survival in his admirer's "powerful rhyme." For Shakespeare, in the tragedies particularly, we are all fools of time, its victims, and I read the famous Sonnet 116 as a pure irony:

> Let me not to the marriage of true minds
> Admit impediments; love is not love
> Which alters where it alteration finds. . . .

How many in the plays then represent a "marriage of true minds"? The best marriage in Shakespeare is that of the Macbeths, an assertion by which I intend no irony, though to call them "true minds" would be sublimely hideous. Shakespeare, unsurpassed in all else, is so advanced in irony that we haven't caught up to him yet. The greatest of all the Sonnets, 129, is perhaps the only poem of the sequence that is beyond irony:

> Th'expense of spirit in a waste of shame
> Is lust in action, and till action, lust
> Is perjured, murd'rous, bloody, full of blame,
> Savage, extreme, rude, cruel, not to trust;
> Enjoyed no sooner but despised straight,
> Past reason hunted, and no sooner had,
> Past reason hated as a swallowed bait
> On purpose laid to make the taker mad:
> Mad in pursuit and in possession so,
> Had, having, and in quest to have, extreme;
> A bliss in proof, and proved, a very woe,
> Before, a joy proposed, behind, a dream.
> >   All this the world well knows yet none knows well
> >   To shun the heaven that leads men to this hell.

Some find Hamlet in this; for me it prophesies a later Shakespeare, beyond *Measure for Measure*. I cannot think of another short poem in the language that moves with the furious energy of Sonnet 129. There are no personnages here, and we are a long way off from the fair youth; it is as though he never was. But the impersonal mode is a defense, perhaps against madness, both of pursuit and of possession. Lear, crying out against the hell of female sexuality, begged for what might sweeten his imagination, knowing that his emotion was insane. Shakespeare, surely at one with this sonnet's speaker, is momentarily and deliberately less sane than the mad old king. As I read later Shakespeare, the vision of Sonnet 129 becomes all but normative in him. I tend to reread "The Phoenix and Turtle" each time I brood on "The expense of spirit in a waste of shame," if only to sweeten my own imagination with Shakespeare at his gentlest:

> Truth may seem, but cannot be,
> Beauty brag, but 'tis not she,
> Truth and Beauty buried be.
>
> To this urn let those repair
> That are either true or fair;
> For these dead birds sigh a prayer.

Biography of
William Shakespeare

(1564–1616)

"He was born at Stratford-upon-Avon,—married, and had children there—went to London where he commenced actor, and wrote poems and plays—returned to Stratford, made his will, died, and was buried. . . . "

That was what George Stevens wrote in the 1766 edition of the Sonnets. We know practically nothing about the private life of the man credited with the best English poetry and drama ever written.

William Shakespeare was baptized on April 26, 1564, in Holy Trinity Church in Stratford-upon-Avon. His birthday is celebrated on April 23, since baptism usually occurred within three or four days of a child's birth. His father, John Shakespeare, made gloves, sold wool, and played a prominent role in local government. He married Mary Arden, of Wilmicote, Warwickshire, in or around 1557. She came from an established family and had inherited some land. William was the third of their of eight children. He attended grammar school in Stratford-upon-Avon, where he learned to read, write, and speak Latin, and where he also studied classical literature and history.

Shakespeare did not go on to university, though. Instead, he married at the age of 18. His bride, Anne Hathaway, was from the nearby village of Shottery. She was eight years Shakespeare's senior, and came from a family who had a beautiful farmhouse two miles from Stratford. There are two dates of interest found in the records of the church in Stratford: the first is May 26, 1583, when his daughter, named Susanna, was baptized, and the second is February 2, 1585, when his twins, Hamnet and Judith, were also baptized. (The son, Hamnet, died 11 years later.)

Virtually nothing is known about the next eight years of Shakespeare's life. There are stories that he poached for deer while on the estate of a local magnate, Sir Thomas Lucy of Charlecote. Legend has it that he was convicted of poaching and forced to leave Stratford, and that he earned his living as a schoolmaster or as a soldier.

Scholars don't know exactly how or when Shakespeare's career in the theater began. But, in 1592, a dramatist named Robert Greene attacked Shakespeare as an "upstart crow" in his pamphlet, *Greene's Groatsworth of Wit.* That indicates that he was by then well known in the literary world of London. His first play, *Henry VI, Part I,* was written and produced in 1589. Soon afterward he wrote the second and third parts of the play.

Shakespeare apparently attracted the attention of nobility who patronized the drama. From 1594 onward he was a member of Lord Chamberlain's Company, a leading theater company that frequently performed at the royal court. (After the ascension of James I to the throne in 1603, the company was called the King's Men). Shakespeare was not only the dramatist for this company, but he also owned a share its operations and was concerned with the financial success of the plays he wrote. He also acted in his plays;

but only in secondary roles, such as the ghost in *Hamlet* and Adam in *As You Like It*. In 1599, the Globe Theater was built in Southwark, giving the company a profitable venue.

Shakespeare prospered early in his career and built his family's fortunes. We know that the coat of arms was granted to him in 1596. He bought properties in Stratford and in London. In 1597, he bought a large Stratford house called New Place. In 1602 he purchased 100 acres of farmland and bought a share of Stratford tithes in 1605.

He had retired from the stage by 1613 and wrote nothing in the last three years of his life. Shakespeare made his will on March 25, 1616. In this long and detailed document, he bequeathed his ample property to the male heirs of his first daughter and the "second best bed" in the house to his wife. No one has ever deciphered the meaning of this strange legacy. He died on April 23, 1616.

Shakespeare devoted himself to his art for 20 years, writing more than a million words of poetry and drama of sublime quality. He published his first poems, *Venus and Adonis* and *The Rape of Lucrece*, in 1593 and 1594, respectively. Both were dedicated to Henry Wriothesley, Earl of Southampton. They are also remarkably free of errors (which is not the case with Shakespeare's plays). Undoubtedly, Shakespeare read the proofs. His 154 sonnets, dedicated to the mysterious "Mr. W.H.," were not published until 1609, but they cover almost 20 years of Shakespeare's life: some of the poems appear to have been composed around 1593, or perhaps even earlier. There is no evidence that Shakespeare participated in their publication.

Shakespeare's 38 plays are divided four categories. The comedies are: *The Comedy of Errors, The Taming of the Shrew, The Two Gentlemen of Verona, A Midsummer Night's Dream, Love's Labour's Lost, The Merchant of Venice, As You Like It, The Merry Wives of Windsor, Much Ado About Nothing, Twelfth Night, Troilus and Cressida, All's Well That Ends Well,* and *Measure for Measure*. The histories are: *Henry the Sixth Part One, Henry the Sixth Parts Two and Three, Richard the Third, King John, Richard the Second, Henry the Fourth Part One, Henry the Fourth Part Two, Henry the Fifth,* and *Henry the Eighth*. The tragedies are: *Titus Andronicus, Romeo and Juliet, Julius Caesar, Hamlet, Othello, King Lear, Macbeth, Antony and Cleopatra, Coriolanus,* and *Timon of Athens*. The romances are: *Pericles, Cymbeline, The Winter's Tale, The Tempest,* and *The Two Noble Kinsmen* (which was written in collaboration with John Fletcher).

The noted Argentine poet and writer Jorge Luis Borges writes about Shakespeare in "Everything and Nothing":

> Before or after his death, he stood face to face with God, he said to Him, "I who, in vain have been so many men, want to be one man— myself." The voice of the Lord answered him out of the whirlwind, "I too have no self; I dreamed the world as you dreamed your work, my Shakespeare, and among the shapes of my dream are you, who, like me, are many men and no one."

There is no more fitting tribute to the Bard, whose plays and poems still fill us with awe. ❁

Analysis of
Shakespeare's Sonnets

Shakespeare's sonnets were published in 1609 by Thomas Thorpe. Shakespeare probably wrote the sonnets over many years, and it seems that he did not oversee their publication. Instead of a dedication by the author, there is only an enigmatic devotion to "Mr. W.H." who is described as "the only begetter" of the sonnets—undersigned with Thomas Thorpe's initials. Scholars do not know who Mr. W.H. was; nor do they know if he was the poet's inspiration.

The English (or Shakespearean) sonnet is written in iambic pentameter (five metrical feet to a line, each foot having one unstressed syllable followed by a stressed syllable), and falls into three quatrains and a rhymed (heroic) couplet for an overall rhyme scheme of abab cdcd efef gg.

Although it cannot be said that the order in which Thorpe printed the 154 sonnets had the Bard's approval, numerous attempts by scholars to rearrange them have failed. In their original order, the first 126 sonnets are addressed to a young nobleman, "a fair youth." Sonnets 127–152 focus on a woman, presumably the poet's mistress, a mysterious "dark lady." Sonnets 153 and 154 are filled with mythological references, but they still discuss the speaker's desire for his mistress.

Shakespeare's sonnets do not tell stories so much as they incarnate the tensions between conflicting urges within the self. As Ernst Robert Curtius superbly said in his book *European Literature and the Latin Middle Ages*:

> The sonnet was the invention of genius. To modulate an erotic theme through hundreds of sonnets was an only too attractive invention of Petrarch's, which spread almost like an epidemic disease and made the sixteenth century sonnet-mad. Shakespeare was able to refill the outworn form with his soul's tensions.

One of Shakespeare's preoccupations appears to have been with the notion of ideal love and how it should stand up to the passage of time. The opening phrase of Sonnet 19, "Devouring time," is derived from the proverb, "Time devours all things." Line 4 ("And burn the long-lived phoenix in her blood") refers to the legend of the phoenix, a bird that was said to have lived for several centuries, died a fiery death, then rose from its own ashes, ready to repeat the cycle. The poet uses the phoenix (an archetypal symbol of immortality) to underscore time's power by stating that even the mythical bird is not immune to its ravages.

The speaker then forbids time from committing "one most heinous crime," (8) which would be to draw lines of age on the face of his beloved: "O carve not with thy hours my love's fair brow,/Nor draw no lines there with thine antique pen" (9–10). The speaker goes on to say that his beloved must remain as he now is in order to preserve the standard of beauty for future generations (11–12).

By the closing couplet, the poet has found a way to triumph over time: he asserts that despite time's "wrong" (13), his love will remain forever young because he is immortalized in verse. The word "love" in the sonnet's final line may denote not only the beloved, but also the poet's own feelings of passion and affection for him: both are now frozen in time by the poet's verse.

Sonnet 53 celebrates the qualities of the beloved that inspire the lover to commemorate him. Let us consider the speaker's wonder at the beloved's very essence:

> What is your substance, whereof are you made
> That millions of strange shadows on you tend?
>
> (1–2)

Two Platonic terms are present here: substance and shadows. Plato (and his adherents in the Renaissance) theorized that perceived reality was not actually real. What we see, they thought, are mere shadows of a thing's true substance. In Sonnet 53, the poet uses the Platonic idea of beauty, saying that his beloved embodies true beauty, from which all other things we perceive as beautiful (shadows of true beauty) derive. The story of Adonis (5), which Shakespeare tells at length in his poem *Venus and Adonis*, is the tale of an ideally beautiful boy with whom Venus falls hopelessly in love. To the lover, even Adonis is "poorly imitated" (6) when compared with his beloved. In fact, all examples of beauty, from Helen of Troy to the spring and harvest seasons, are present in the youth's own all-encompassing, transcendent beauty (7–12).

The last line of the sonnet, "But you like none, none you, for constant heart," distinguishes the beloved from things of mere "external grace" (13) by virtue of his inner, personal grace.

Sonnet 55 revisits the idea of poetry as the key to immortality. Shakespeare follows a poetic convention that can be traced back to classical antiquity in Homer, Pindar, Virgil, and Horace. This sonnet echoes an ode by Horace, in which he says that he has created a monument more lasting than bronze through his verse. In keeping with Horace, the poet says that no monument will outlive his "powerful rhyme" (2), and that his beloved will shine more brightly in these lines than by an inscription on "unswept stone" (4), which will become dirty with neglect and the passage of time. Pointless warfare can overturn statues, and riotous fighting can obliterate the stonemason's handiwork (5–6). But neither Mars's warlike sword, the poet says, nor the fires of war (the sword and fire traditionally represent destruction) can demolish this "living record" (in verse form) of the beloved's memory (7–8).

Because the beloved has now been immortalized in Sonnet 55, his memory will go on, despite death and the brutally indifferent forces of nature. Future generations will continue singing his praises until the absolute end of the world (10–12). The closing couplet refers to the Christian idea of the Last Judgment, the time for universal resurrection of the dead. Until Judgment Day, the poet says, the beloved will live on in his poetry, and, therefore, "in lovers' eyes" as well (14).

Sonnet 87 does not aspire to immortality (or anything else beyond venting the speaker's immediate disillusionment with love. The first line, "Farewell, thou art too dear for my possessing," could mean that the poet is readily giving up his beloved, or that he has no choice in the matter, but is reluctantly letting him go. The poet is saying that his beloved is too precious—and costly (note the play on the word "dear")—to keep. The force of the young man's special qualities, "the charter of [his] worth" (3) is enough to set him free. Therefore, the speaker's ties to the beloved are "determinate" (4), begun or ended by the beloved's choice. The lover insists on his unworthiness: "For how do I hold thee but by thy granting,/ And for that riches where is my deserving?" (5–6). At first, readers may be surprised by this self-abnegation on the speaker's part, since it is hard to imagine that Shakespeare was unaware of his own genius (Pequigney).

But the speaker's exaggerated sense of the beloved's worth against his own sense of lowliness, combined with his heavy use of commercial language ("estimate," "charter," "gift," "patent," "misprision") suggests bitter sarcasm. The poet may also be using dry, emotionless legal terminology in an attempt to tolerate the painful instability of desire.

In the closing couplet, the illusory king who finds himself to be "no such matter" (14) upon awakening is usually thought to be the disillusioned speaker. Other interpretations, however, suggest that perhaps the speaker saw the beloved as a king, then realized him to be no such thing in the aftermath of their separation.

Sonnet 94 implicitly warns the "fair youth" to be fair and pure of heart. The poet states that those in a position to hurt others who refrain from doing so, those who can lead others but remain uncorrupted are the rightful heirs to "heaven's graces" (5). "Heaven's graces" may mean good fortune granted by God. In line 6, "And husband nature's riches from expense," "nature's riches" may be a sexual reference.

Those individuals of character described in the first six lines of the sonnet are self-possessed in their purity; others are only excellence's occasional keepers ("stewards"), rather than its true and constant possessors (7–8). People of genuine excellence live and die seemingly unaware of their unique place in the world, much as a summer flower is unaware of its beauty (9–10). If individuals of distinguished moral character succumb to "base infection" (11), however, it runs deeper than the corruption of lesser persons because it is unexpected (13–14).

According to Stephen Booth's interpretation, Sonnet 116 is basically concerned with the constant nature of true love. The poet gives the sonnet a somewhat psalm-like opening by using the word "let" in the first line: "Let me not to the marriage of true minds/Admit impediments" (1–2). The sonnet as a whole reads like a set of vows.

The poet achieves a positive definition of love through a series of negative assertions: "Love is not love" (2), "Love's not time's fool (9), "Love alters not with his brief hours and weeks" (11). He uses images of stability to further define love: "an ever fixed mark/that looks on tempest and is never shaken" (5–6), and "the star to every wand'ring barque [ship]" (7).

Although "Love's not time's fool" (9), the poet reminds us that love must withstand the eventual decline of physical beauty when it comes within the sweep of time's "bending sickle [sic]" (10).

The sonnet ends with another negative assertion:

> If this be error and upon me proved,
> I never writ, nor no man ever loved.
>
> (13–14)

The poem's very existence, the lover asserts, is sufficient proof of ideal love's existence.

Sonnet 129 is the only example discussed here that examines the lover's relationship with his mistress. In the opening lines, "Th' expense of spirit in a waste of shame/Is lust in action," the poet states that the pursuit of sexual gratification is a disgraceful misallocation of vital energy. The word "action" in this case denotes sexual activity. The passion that drives the pursuit of sex, however, is "perjured, murd'rous, bloody, full of blame,/savage, extreme, rude, cruel, not to trust" (3–4). The speaker explodes with disgust against the pursuit of women by men and at women's enticement of them ("On purpose laid to make the taker mad" [8]). As soon as the passion is satisfied, he says, it is immediately regretted: "Enjoyed no sooner but despised straight" (5). What is anticipated as pure joy soon becomes "a very woe" once it is enacted (11).

The poet ends the sonnet by concluding that despite bitter experience, men will never be immune to the sexual allure of women:

> All this the world well knows, yet none knows well
> To shun the heav'n that leads men to this hell.
>
> (13–14)

The speaker's outpouring of disgust and self-reproach concerning women is notable in contrast to his more romantic treatment of his feelings for the male beloved. ❀

Critical Views on

Sonnet 19

JOSEPH PEQUIGNEY ON THE POET'S RELATIONSHIP WITH TIME

[Joseph Pequigney is Professor of English at the State University of New York at Stony Brook. In his book *Such Is My Love: A Study of Shakespeare's Sonnets*, from which this extract is taken, Pequigney argues that the sonnet sequence represents "the grand masterpiece of homoerotic poetry." He describes a complex and psychologically realistic story of the poet's erotic attachment to the fair young man of Sonnets 1–126. Sonnets 127–154, dealing with the dark lady, are read as a footnote to the jealousy crisis described in sonnets 40–42. The first 126 sonnets depict a sexual relationship between the poet and the youth that complies with Freud's views on homosexuality.]

Sonnet 19 is an apostrophe to "Devouring Time." It is the first poem that does not directly address the youth (neither does Sonnet 5, but this is hardly an exception, since it forms a double sonnet with Sonnet 6, which does); he is referred to here as "my love." The poet is acting on his commitment at 15.3, to be "all in war with Time for love of you" (that phrase might almost serve as a title for Sonnet 19), when he challenges, in an effort to keep his friend intact, the universal devourer. He begins, bravely enough, with a series of imperatives, one to a line through 19.6, but they are concessive, since they simply direct Time to "do whate'er thou wilt . . . To the wide world and all her fading sweets." A reversal occurs at 19.8 with the command, "But I forbid thee one most heinous crime," the savaging of "my love." Yet the bold and forceful command gives way in the third quatrain to the milder, rather imploring, tones of "O carve not," "Nor draw no lines there [= wrinkles on the forehead] with thine antique pen," and "Him . . . untainted do allow." That the protector becomes aware that his effort is fruitless is made evident in a second reversal at 19.13: "Yet do thy worst, old Time: despite thy wrong," where both "thy worst" and "wrong" are equivalent to "most heinous crime" above. The speaker returns to the concessive imperative, now resigned to the fact that the youth, though he might serve as "beauty's pattern to succeeding men," will not be spared. "Time," after being characterized first as monstrously "Devouring," then neutrally as "swift-footed," becomes simply "old" in 19.13, the adjective implying an almost affable attitude toward him just when we might expect the greatest disagreement. The attitude is accounted for by the last line, where a third reversal occurs: "despite thy wrong / My love shall in my verse ever live young." There is, after all, a recourse available to the poet for keeping "old Time" at bay and his beloved alive. Distinctions of a semiparadoxical nature are latent in the couplet: the protagonist's words as apostrophized utterance fail to deter time, but words organized into poetry will do the job; the youth cannot escape decay in his human actuality but can do so in his existence as an aesthetic object; verse cannot prevent the deleterious effects of time (and his "antique pen") on the freshness of "my love," but his fresh beauty will be beyond the reach of time once it has been recreated in verse.

For the space now of five sonnets, 15–19, poetry, in its capacity to confer the perennial life on its subject, is the continuous text. The persona comes out as a poet, abruptly, at the end of Sonnet 15, to take upon himself the formidable task of doing "war with Time" as champion of the vulnerable other, and he does so out of "love for thee" — the motivation that underlies the subsequent immortalizing sonnets. It does not matter that the idea of reproduction briefly returns in Sonnet 16 to cast doubt on his enterprise, since, after Sonnet 17, that idea can be discarded once and for all.

The steps taken by Shakespeare's persona in the opening movement of the sonnets may now, in summary, be retraced. From the start, as throughout Part I, he is preoccupied with the imposing beauty of the youth. His first reaction is that beauty requires reproduction and that the youth should find some woman and breed, even though he, the giver of this counsel, has little to urge in favor of women, marriage, family life, or heterosexual gratification. Next, this bodily beauty, together with affection on the part of its possessor, elicits love in the speaker. He thereupon idealizes the friend, first by ascribing to him a "presence . . . gentle and kind" in Sonnet 10 and then virtue—the "truth" in Sonnet 14 and "inward worth" in 16; and this new esteem for the friend's disposition and character is the result rather than the cause of love. Moreover, faults are no longer imputed to him — never after Sonnet 11, and even this sonnet is a temporary throwback to an earlier stage, a retreat that follows upon and briefly suspends the sudden emergence of love. Finally, love prompts the poet to essay an alternative means of salvaging the beloved, a means solely at his command and independent of the biological means that would require the youth to beget children on one of those eager maidens. The adoption of eternalizing rhyme as the vehicle, enabling exclusive interaction between the maker and the receiving subject, suggests an intensification of the protagonist's love and, as it is born of and nourished by beauty, its amorous character.

And what do the nineteen sonnets say about the stages through which their recipient passes? He is certainly not persuaded to breed. Instead of following the instructions to do so, he takes increasing interest in the instructor. The narcissistic impulses perceptible at 1.5–6 and elsewhere in the initial stage seem to undergo modification; he appears to change over from being self-involved to being involved with his praiser. This inference is supported by the fact that the last allusion to his autoeroticism occurs just before, and none occurs after, the emergence of love in Sonnet 10, line 13 of which makes the first mention of his "love of me."

Keeping in mind Plato's conception of love, in the Symposium, as desire for the everlasting possession of the beautiful, we may perceive the following psychological states as those the protagonist undergoes in the course of falling in love: (1) his desire for the hereditary continuation of the youth's beauty; (2) his desire for the genetic survival of his beautiful friend; and (3) his desire to render his beloved everlasting in poetry. A fourth stage is inaugurated in Sonnet 20, and it consists of a passionate desire for the person of the youthful beauty, with the erotic love to keep on yielding up, periodically, eternalizations in rhyme.

—Joseph Pequigney, *Such Is My Love.* (Chicago: University of Chicago Press, 1985), pp. 27–28.

☙

JOEL FINEMAN ON POETRY AND PROGENY IN THE SONNETS

[Joel Fineman, Professor of English Literature at the University of California at Berkeley, is the author of *Shakespeare's Perjured Eye* (1986) and *The Subjectivity Effect in Western Literary Tradition* (1991). Fineman accepts the traditional division of the sonnets: 1–126 addressed to a young man, and 127–154 addressed to the dark lady. He argues that in the Sonnets, Shakespeare creates a new poetic subjectivity, a new poetics and a new first-person. The Sonnets also become a point of departure for thoughts about gender, and the nature of modern subjectivity.]

[T]here is a specific *materiality* that complements the way the young man sonnets break from the poetics of the ideal complementarity. On the one hand, from the very beginning of the sequence, the poet's diction and his broadest concerns recall traditional epideictic things, but they do so in such an odd and eccentric way that these apparently very familiar images become themselves, in their very phenomenality, examples of the way the artifacts of praise no longer are the same.

This is most clearly apparent in the imagery used to develop the initial procreation argument, an argument that is thematically unprecedented in the genre of the sonnet sequence, but that is nevertheless both like and unlike all that comes before. Thus the poet's young man is supposed to be the model of the ideal, with all the force and resonance that "model" carries in and idealist metaphysics. The young man is the exemplar, the form, the type, the *eidos,* of "kind," of all subsidiary virtues. Rather, he is the exemplar of all exemplifications, the Form of forms, the Type of types, the very Idea of the ideal. The Neo-Platonic presuppositions at stake in such a conception are clear enough, and it would be possible to cite innumerable sonneteering parallels to the way the young man, as beloved, is "the pattern of all those" "figures of delight" (98) or to the was he is "beauty's pattern to succeeding men" (19). Despite the peculiarity of his gender, therefore, the young man is presented in an immediately recognizable literary context. Like a Beatrice or a Laura or a Stella, the young man stands, or is supposed to stand, both for a singularly perfect nature and for the yet more total perfection of the Nature of nature. As "beauty's rose" (1) he represents not only the particular token and the general type of ideality, but, also, at the same time, the harmoniously organic way these two are related to each other. The eternizing themes of the procreation argument—which, outside the conventions of the amatory sonnet, are old themes, going back at least to Cicero—translate this familiar ontology into the terms of what is an equally familiar biology, fleshing out a half-Platonic and half-Aristotelian categorical logic of genera and species by referring it to, or explaining it with, the reproductive generations of replicating human kind each generation repeating the generation it succeeds. In a straightforward way, therefore, the opening young man sonnets stress the familial likeness of "like father, like son" by reapplying well-known conceits of ideal likeness, of "Ideas Mirrour." And it is easy for them to do so, for it is a metaphysical as well as physical imperative that "your sweet issue your sweet form should bear" (13).

Perhaps this was the only way that Shakespeare could have so readily adapted the heterosexual tradition of the Petrarchist sonnet to the exegencies of poetic address to a man. Or perhaps, as has been suggested by several critics, Shakespeare really was commissioned to exhort a patron's son to marriage, and he therefore seized upon the procreation theme as a uniquely appropriate sonneteering means with which to accomplish this serviceable end. Whatever the reason, it remains the case that it is only because there is so perfect a fit between the metaphysics of resemblance, as developed by traditional poetics, and the physiology of resemblance, as developed by traditional biology, that the poet's arguments for procreation carry any literary weight at all. Only in such an idealist context can we understand how the young man's young man initiates what is to be the eternal repetition of the young man's sameness. Only in the context of the kind of idealism for which time is "the moving image of eternity," as Plato describes it in the Timaeus, does the young man's progeny become the temporal unfolding of the young man's timeless permanence. Only if we grant the unitary arithmetic of idealism does it make sense that the young man, multiplying himself after his own kind, will father the "many" that will prove him "One." And only if we accept the tidy categoriality of genus and species will we understand how the young man spawns a series of particulars whose lineal succession embodies the young man's universality: "Proving his beauty by succession thine" (2).

And, as I have said, as with the characterization of progeny, so with the characterization of poetry. By comparing his own epideictic verse to the young man's procreated issue the poet is able to modulate in the opening sonnets from advising the young man "to breed another thee" (6), who will "leave thee living in posterity," to boasting instead about the way "my love will in my verse ever live young" (19). To be sure, the exact relationship developed between poetry and progeny varies in the course of the series, so that sometimes poetry and progeny are opposed to each other, as in sonnet 16, where "my barren rhyme" is unflatteringly compared to "your living flowers," whereas elsewhere—this is the more frequent case—the two are instead identified with each other, as in sonnet 17: "But were some child of yours alive that time, / You should live twice, in it and in my rhyme." Quite apart from these explicit comments, however, there is from the beginning of the procreation series, which is the beginning of the sequence as a whole, a consistent and an insistent figural equating of the poet's verse with the young man's "succession," the effect of which is that we readily think of the one as the example of the other. Thus the young man's young man is an immortalizing flower, as, for example, the issue of the ever-renewable "beauty's rose" of sonnet 1, or he is the alternative to the "totter'd weed" of sonnet 2, or he is "flowers distill'd" in sonnet 5, and all of this floral imagery prepares us for the way the gardening poet, speaking about his poetry, will subsequently say: "And all in war with Time for love of you, / As he takes from you, I ingraft you new" (15). Similarly, to take the visual image which I have most discussed, the young man's young man is his father's vivifying image, as in "die single, and thine image dies with thee" (3), so that later poetry itself can become the young man's animating mirror, as in: "So long as men can breathe or eyes can see, / So long lives this, and this gives life to thee" (18).

—Joel Fineman, *Shakespeare's Perjured Eye*. (Berkeley: University of California Press, 1986), pp. 250–252.

℘

HELEN VENDLER ON THE ALTERED NATURE OF TIME IN SONNET 19

[Helen Vendler is the A. Kingsley Porter University Professor at Harvard University. Her previous books include *Yeats' Vision and the Later Plays* (1963) and *On Extended Wings: Wallace Stevens' Longer Poems* (1969). Her most recent book is *The Art of Shakespeare's Sonnets* (1997), from which this extract is taken.]

Whether or not the poem is fundamentally incoherent, it is interesting in the chaos of its multiple senses of Time's powers. To begin with the proverbial and Ovidian topos of devouring Time is conventional enough, but Time is soon seen doing very odd things. The might of Time is emphasized, but not in the usual way; in other sonnets, Time does what is natural to it (it overthrows monuments, etc.), but here it does, in the first quatrain, exclusively *un*natural things, de-lionizing the lion, de-tigerizing the tiger, de-maternalizing Mother Earth, and de-immortalizing the phoenix. These are *not* devourings—nor are they things that, in the normal course of time, Time does; and *contra Naturam* is one of the most powerful accusations available to Shakespeare's Renaissance speaker.

We must deduce that even Time is not allowed these acts in the ordinary governed course of Nature; a lion with blunted paws, a devouring Gaia, a toothless tiger, and a mortal phoenix would each be a *lusus Naturae*. Such acts on Time's part would be crimes against Nature, as making lions grow old, e.g., would not be. We are to deduce that the young man, as beauty's *pattern*, would in the course of things be naturally exempt, as a Platonic form (a being nobler even than the phoenix), from Time's destruction. Consequently, the *most heinous crime* is not per se the wrinkling of a young man's brow, but the destruction of one of the forms that Nature needs as patterns to create more creatures from: *She carved thee for her seal, and meant thereby / Thou shouldst print more*, said the version putting the responsibility of self-reproduction on the young man (sonnet 11), but here the responsibility for the perpetuation of the pattern is shifted to Nature and Time.

The second quatrain attempts to do Shakespearean justice to Time, by admitting that in its *swift[ness]*, (the quality dominating Q₂) it makes *glad* as well as sorry *seasons*. But this brief impulse of justice toward the adversary does not extend to indulging the crime of form-destruction. It is because the contemplated crime against the young man is the destruction of form that Time is suddenly transformed into an artist—a sculptor and then a painter, defacing Nature's masterpiece with his *antique pen*. *Untainted*— resembling antique in some phonetic respects—also suggests, in the context *pen* and *pattern*, the word *unpainted*, and will in fact seem to "generate" *painted* in sonnet 20. We now see that the Ovidian epithet *devouring* applies properly only to the envisaged disappearance of the beloved.

The couplet (with its implied contrast between corporeal life and life in verse) suggests that physical pattern-destruction is indeed, and always had been, within old Time's power. The pattern of beauty may indeed be destroyed in embodied Nature by an unnatural crime committed by a false artist, Time; yet language can preserve the pattern that flesh has forgotten. (It is not necessary to imagine, as Kerrigan does, that time's *worst* is the actual death of the young man; his death would be anticlimactic, since it is his beauty, as pattern, which is the precious form of which the destruction would be time's worst act.)

The almost blustering bravado of uttering, in the face of Time, both positive concessions (*blunt, make, pluck, burn,* etc.) and negative commands (*I forbid thee . . . carve not . . . draw no lines*) must, of course, subside. *Yet do thy worst* ("even if you do the worst you can") allows the transition from the realm of flesh to the realm of art, as defeat conceded in one sphere (the commanding of Time) is avoided by triumph in another (living verse).

The notion that Nature makes a mental pattern and then replicates it in the flesh is fancifully mythologized in the following sonnet, 20. In 19 it is taken for granted rather than made explicit, and the imaginative effort expended on pattern-creation in 20 is here spent on the great hard words, with their frequent trochaic or spondaic emphasis: *blunt, paws, brood, pluck, keen, teeth, tiger's jaws, burn, blood. Devouring Time. . . the earth devour. . . with thy hours* tolls the progression that turns *devouring Time* to *swift-footed* Time and then to old Time; by the end all values have been jettisoned except beauty's pattern, *young* in verse.

—Helen Vendler, *The Art of Shakespeare's Sonnets*. (Cambridge, MA: Harvard University Press, 1997), pp. 124–126.

Sonnet 53

Hilton Landry on Platonism's Influence on Sonnet 53

[Hilton Landry (1924) was a professor of English at Kent State University who published *Interpretations in Shakespeare's Sonnets* (1963) and *The Marriage of True Minds: Truth and Error in Sonnet 116* (1967).]

Sonnet 53, because of its diction and provenience, might be called the most Platonic of the Sonnets. Universally regarded as a piece of unqualified praise, it exhibits the following structure: a Platonic generalization in the first quatrain is illustrated by particulars in the second and third; the twelfth line, which gives a rough summary of the sense, is restated by the thirteenth, while the last line presents a novel climax.

> What is your substance, whereof you are made,
> That millions of strange shadows on you tend?
> Since every one hath, every one, one shade,
> And you, but one, can every shadow lend.
> Describe Adonis, and the counterfeit
> Is poorly imitated after you.
> On Helen's cheek all art of beauty set,
> And in you Grecian tires are painted new.
> Speak of the spring and foison of the year:
> The one doth shadow of your beauty show,
> The other as your bounty doth appear,
> And you in every blessed shape we know.
> In all external grace you have some part,
> But you like none, none you, for constant heart.

The opening quatrain, depending on the distinction between shadow and substance as well as various senses of shadow, has Shakespeare asking the handsome youth, What is your essence, what makes you what you are, that millions of images not your own serve or wait on you? For everyone has only one shadow, and you, though but one person, can give rise to every image (of the millions which serve you). For example, describe Adonis, and the world picture of that perfect male turns out to be a poor imitation of you; enhance Helen's natural beauty as much as possible, and you are represented anew in Grecian attire (ll. 5–8). Or speak of spring and of autumn, season of plenty; spring seems the image of your beauty, fall of your generosity. Indeed, we recognize you in every form blessed with beauty (ll. 9–12). You have some share in all eternal beauty (for you are in a sense its Idea), but you are like no one, and no one is like you, in regard to constancy of heart.

"Substance" signifies the essence or the nature of a thing, "*quod stat subtus*, that which stands beneath, and (as it were) supports, the appearance"; also, in accordance with the expansion in the last half of the line, it denotes the material of which something is made. "Shadow" plays on several senses: body's silhouette (the "shade" of l. 3); image, reflection, likeness; and picture or portrait (the "counterfeit" of l. 5). In Plato's *Symposium*

(212a) the difference between the Idea of Beauty, which is sole and absolute, and all other beauties is put in terms of the disparity between substance and shadow, truth and mere images or reflections of it; and "shadow" is virtually a technical term of the Neoplatonism of Shakespeare's time:

> 'Shadow' and 'reflexion' were used by renaissance Platonists as alternative metaphors in expounding Plato's doctrine that Beauty which we see is the copy of an eternal pattern—Giordano Bruno had discoursed in Paris *De Umbris Idearum* . . .

In short, the poem's principal conceit, that all *external* beauty consists of mere shadows of the youth's "perfect" Beauty, may derive from metaphysical Platonism. This conceit is ostensibly enriched by the attribution of bounty and transcended or made even more Platonic in the last line by the attribution of unique constancy.

Although in one sense the liberality of the handsome youth is explained by the fourth line — he lends all the images of his beauty that the poet sees — the sphere in which his bounty operates is not otherwise defined. But with "foison" as its "image," his generosity inevitably recalls Antony, who was generous as lover, friend, and ruler: "For his bounty, / There was no winter in't, an autumn 'twas / That grew the more by reaping" (*Antony and Cleopatra*, V.ii. 86–88). These lines in turn remind us of Juliet, whose bounty was also infinite, though restricted to the sphere of love: "My bounty is as boundless as the sea, / My love as deep; the more I give to thee, / The more I have, for both are infinite" (*Romeo and Juliet*, II.ii. 133–135). One assumes, then, that the youth is generous in the personal relations of friendship and love, which is highly commendable and desirable as long as he is constant; but as the sexual implications of "liberal," "frank," and "free" may suggest, giving freely and generously of oneself is also a necessary condition of inconstancy.

The fact that bounty may not be a pure blessing is hardly enough to justify the qualms one is likely to feel about taking the last line at its face value. Nor is it enough to be "struck by the inapplicability of this tribute to the personage addressed in 35, 40–42, and others." Still, one is inclined to suspect that there is unconscious irony in the assertion and to ask, Why talk about constancy; isn't it usually taken for granted — when it actually exists? The answer is not to be found in J.B. Leishman's suggestion of a conventional borrowing from Ronsard:

> Despite the 'conventional' allusions to Adonis and Helen in Shakespeare's sonnet, I must confess that I have always been rather surprised by the conventional triteness of the concluding couplet. . . . Why just here should Shakespeare 'drag in' (as one might be inclined to say) the all too familiar 'constant heart'? Perhaps because he had this sonnet of Ronsard's in mind:
>
> Icy un coeur constant, qu'on ne peut esbranler.

Contexts within the absence group furnish answers to this question and some justification of one's doubts, for when the poet's hyperbolic statement is examined in the light of Sonnets 48, 49, 52, 54, and 56–58, one must conclude that it probably springs less from an attitude of confident assurance than from one of fearful hope.

—Hilton Landry, *Interpretations in Shakespeare's Sonnets*. (Berkeley: University of California Press, 1963), pp. 47–50.

๑

Murray Krieger on the Friend as Both One and Many in the Sonnets

[Murray Krieger was Professor of English at the University of California in Los Angeles until 1982. He is the author of *The Tragic Vision: Variations on a Theme in Literary Interpretation* (1960), *The Play and Place of Criticism* (1967), *The Classic Vision: The Retreat from Extremity in Modern Literature* (1971) and *Poetic Presence and Illusion: Essays in Critical History and Theory*. He is also the author of *A Window to Criticism: Shakespeare's Sonnets and Modern Poetics*, from which this extract is taken. Krieger suggests that Shakespeare's Sonnets comprise a "memorial tomb of love to which, as a womb, it gives eternal life" (193). He finds in the Sonnets a key to the nature of poetry and poetics, and focuses on their mirror-window metaphorical system.]

Here the terms are rather "substance" and "shadows," which we should remember from their important role in Sonnet 37 (line 10). The opening question of Sonnet 53 expresses just the mystery that we have seen eluding the answers of our normal reason: what sort of substance can it be which, instead of casting a single shadow, becomes the sole reality attended by "millions of strange shadows"? (The singularity of all but the friend is insisted upon in the four uses of "one" in lines 3–4.) In what follows it becomes clear that there is and has been no other substance, that all is thrust into the friend's shadow. Even the most beautiful creatures turn out to be not originals but mere counterfeits of the single Platonic perfection that was to come and finally to attain worldly existence. We are back, with a certain tightening of metaphor, to the transfigured "praises" of "ladies dead and lovely knights" that allowed Sonnet 106 similarly to transform history into eschatology. We should be reminded also of Sonnets 67–68, in which the insubstantial, imitative world, with its "roses of shadow," is scornfully juxtaposed to the friend's rich and original beauty which is the sole living repository of substantive truth. Or there is Sonnet 113 ("Since I left you, mine eye is in my mind"), in which the entire phenomenal world is transformed for the poet through the intervening presence of the friend which "shapes" that world to himself. Here in Sonnet 113 the friend affects what phenomenal reality can be for the eyes of love, as in the others he affects historical reality in the same way. In all of them the friend, as mirror-window, is—like the Christian Trinity—at once one and many: as substantive entity he is seen as the unique substance that absorbs all entities and reduces the others to shadows of himself. Consequently, the myriads of history and of the phenomenal world are reduced to images struggling in their individual incompleteness to achieve their reality in him. In Sonnet 53 the friend's unitary truth absorbs the natural world as well as the historical process. Springtime and harvest are also reflections of him, so that the poet, in lines 12 and 13, can make his most extravagant claim for this single incarnation of the numberless manifestations of beauty ("And you in every blessed shape we know. / In all external grace you have some part").

—Murray Krieger, *A Window to Criticism: Shakespeare's Sonnets and Modern Poetics.* (Princeton, NJ: Princeton University Press, 1964), pp. 177–178.

⊕

STEPHEN BOOTH ON THE ROLE OF PARADOX IN SONNET 53

[Stephen Booth, Professor of English at the University of California in Berkeley, is the author of *An Essay on Shakespeare's Sonnets, The Book Called Holinshed's Chronicles,* and the editor of *Shakespeare's Sonnets.* Booth demonstrates the organization of Shakespeare's sonnets as a multitude of coexisting but conflicting patterns. The sonnets depend upon a conflict between what is said and what the reader expects.]

I take the time to labor the distinction between our response to a paradox and our response to a paradoxical situation, because I think it is the essential distinction between Shakespeare's sonnets and other poems of similar substance. If I were to say that sonnet 53 is a tissue of paradoxes, I doubt that any reader of the poem would object. Even granting that an audience conditioned to modern criticism is likely to assent blandly to any statement with the phrase *tissue of* in it, it is strange that the truth of this statement should be so easy to accept and so hard to demonstrate. Except for the second sentence (*Since every one hath, every one, one shade, / And you, but one, can every shadow lend*), there is no paradox in the poem that can be satisfactorily restated in prose, and even that exception is doubtful.

As a paraphrase of the second sentence, the following statement is more satisfying than it should be: "one person can only have one shadow; you have many shadows." The paraphrase is a paradox, a paradoxical situation described, pinned down, understood as inexplicable. My paraphrase, like most paradoxes, gives solidity to the situation it describes by means of extralogical form: the verb *have* is repeated in the contrasting clauses; *one,* repeated in the first clause, is set against *many* in the second; *shadows,* the last word of the second clause, balances *shadow,* the last word of the first, and, paired as they are, the singular form and the plural form of the same word capsule the paradoxical situation so that it is an acceptably defined exception within the pale of human logic.

The lines themselves, on the other hand, haven't the simplicity of form or the simplicity of meaning of the paraphrase. To take meaning first, here is an explication of lines 2 through 4 given in 1918 by C. K. Pooler in his Arden edition of the sonnets: the lines, he says, are

> based on a pun: shadow (shade l.3) is (1) the silhouette formed by a body that intercepts the sun's rays; (2) a picture, reflection, or symbol. 'Tend' means Attend, follow as a servant, and is strictly appropriate to 'shadow' only in the first sense, though shadow is used here in the second. . . . All men have one shadow each, in the first sense; you being only one can yet cast many shadows, in the second sense; for everything good and beautiful is either a representation of you or a symbol of your merits.

Pooler achieves the comfort of mastery over these lines not by composing their substance into a paradox but by analyzing them into submission to human understanding. He, too, oversimplifies: a third meaning of *shade* and *shadow* also functions in the first quatrain. Where the substance of a being is in doubt, there is a strong probability that that being is supernatural. The very idea of millions of strange shadows sounds supernatural, and the idea that these shadows tend, "follow as a servant," the being whose nature is under consideration brings with it suggestions of occult practices in which spirits dance attendance on a witch or magician. Line 3, of course, puts to rest any such suggestions by implying that *shadows* in line 2 meant not spirits but "silhouettes formed by a body that intercepts the sun's rays." However, the word *shadow* is replaced by the word *shade*, the most sinister of its synonyms and the one best calculated to reinforce the occult suggestions the rest of the line has suppressed. Pooler's paraphrase is a satisfying critical performance, but once add my suggestions about ghosts to it and the paraphrase becomes so complicated that it defeats its own purpose. One is again in doubt what it is that these lines say and how it is that that is said.

Pooler's explication is formally reinforced by the carefully numbered meanings of *shadow*. My statement of lines 3 and 4 as a paradox (which, by the way, is valid even though Pooler's equally valid paraphrase explains it away) has a similar formal substance from its repetitions of key words and its parallel clause structure. Both Pooler's analysis and my paradox have a formal solidity that makes them mentally graspable. They are defined, static; their internal dynamics are fixed; they are like physical things. What about the lines themselves?

> What is your substance, whereof you are made,
> That millions of strange shadows on you tend?
> Since every one hath, every one, one shade,
> And you, but one, can every shadow lend.

Obviously, the quatrain has formal integrity in its completed rhyme pattern, but there is something else about the quatrain that gives it the firmness of a paradox or an analysis. The words *one* and *every* are repeated much as *shadow* is in my paradox, but, although they present a complication and define it, that complication is gratuitous. The lines as they are sound like a paradox; the play on *every* and *one* gives a paradox-like solidity of form to "everybody, each person, hath one shade and you, a single individual, can every shadow lend." But the machinery of formal paradox is not applied to the paradoxical condition. The lines sound like a paradox, a petrified dilemma, but they are not. The dilemma is still active.

There are three meanings of *shadow* in the quatrain, and as the reader moves from word to word, his mind jumps from one pattern of understanding to another; the jumps are small ones, but there are many of them. The reader's mind is in the state of constant motion appropriate not to paradoxes or poems but to the actual experience of a paradoxical situation.

—Stephen Booth, *An Essay on Shakespeare's Sonnets.* (New Haven, CT: Yale University Press, 1969), pp. 96–110.

✤

JOSEPH PEQUIGNEY ON THE CASE AGAINST PLATONISM IN SONNET 53

[Joseph Pequigney is Professor of English at the State University of New York at Stony Brook. Pequigney argues that the sonnet sequence represents "the grand masterpiece of homoerotic poetry." He describes a complex and psychologically realistic story of the poet's erotic attachment to the fair young man of Sonnets 1–126. Sonnets 127–154, dealing with the dark lady, are read as a footnote to the jealousy crisis described in sonnets 40–42. The first 126 sonnets depict a sexual relationship between the poet and the youth that complies with Freud's views on homosexuality.]

This discourse upon shadows has rather to do with "love's philosophy" than Plato's. The central conceit rests on the everyday observation that "every one," person or thing, casts one and its own shadow. However, the friend is unique, seemingly composed of some unheard-of "substance," since not one but "millions. . . of shadows"—"strange" ones, other than his own—attend him. To the poet's mind all beautiful phenomena, human and other, in art and nature, are shadows of the beautiful beloved. The conception is not Platonic because the "substance" shadowed is a particular physical body and cannot mean "yourself as archetypal Idea," since, in that case, shadows would not be "strange" but regular and expected reflections.

Out of the "millions," four shadows are specified, two from art and mythology in the second quatrain (Adonis, Helen) and two from the seasonal cycles of nature in the third (spring, autumn). Adonis and Helen present these contrasts: one is male, one female; the "counterfeit" of the first is a verbal depiction unrestricted as to bodily parts, and the second is "painted," but only her head, as is indicated by the details of "cheek" and "Grecian tires" (= headdress); each is a paragon of "external graces" (53.13), he that of the handsome youth, she that of feminine beauty; the one is famous for shunning seduction (by Venus), the other for yielding to it (by Paris). The youth is told that artistic delineations of Adonis and Helen are but "shadows," that is, images "poorly imitated after you." This superlative compliment to the more resplendent Adonis-Helen recalls Sonnet 20, where a "woman's face," like Helen's in a painting, is ascribed to him, together with the masculine form ("hue") of an Adonis. Once again, this time with allusions to classical myths, the Master Mistress is portrayed as embodying features of both sexes.

Yet other implications may attach Shakespeare's choice of these particular figures to serve as comparisons. "Describe Adonis," he writes, and he has done so, in the descriptive details scattered through *Venus and Adonis*. That poem, if elucidative of the allusion here, makes it tempting to infer that the friend, sharing more than beauty with Adonis, is likewise unsusceptible to eros. But he is then immediately likened to Helen, who to the contrary showed herself only too susceptible to erotic enticement. The indifference in the one case is to a female, the attraction in the other is to a male; the youth would harbor tendencies akin to those of both mythic figures if he turned out sexually to be indifferent to women and attracted to men. That interesting possibility will be explored further, but the failure of the earlier persuasions to breed might here be pertinently recalled.

In the third quatrain of Sonnet 53, where each "shadow" is seasonal, that of the spring shows "your beauty," the lovely season being assigned the same function as the Adonis and Helen. The autumnal "foison" has a different function, for in it a new quality, "your bounty," appears. The word "bounty" means 'generosity with something abundantly possessed.' That 'something' is certainly not a fortune, as those who suppose the poems to be concerned with patronage would have it. In annotating 53.1 Ingram and Redpath give, among other definitions of "substance," that of 'wealth,' adding, parenthetically, 'he has many servant shadows to attend him.' *Millions* of them? And just how could 'wealth' be imagined to cast "shadows"? A.L. Rowse comments, "I think we may infer that the poet [Shakespeare] had been the recipient of his patron's [Southampton's] bounty." Such readings stem from the presumption that the friend is a nobleman. To the contrary, his "bounty" consists not in dispensing funds but rather in yielding the richness of his physical beauty to his lover, of giving himself personally and sexually, and this sense accords with the commendation of him at the end of Sonnet 52, where his "worthiness"—not financial worth but corporal excellence—admits of "triumph" when he is carnally "had."

Lines 12 and 13 of Sonnet 53 express, in different words, the very same idea, that "you" appear "in every blessed shape" and participate "in all external grace," both phrases making reference to the visually beautiful. The last line, by contrast, extols the friend for a virtue that is interior and unshared: "But you, like none, none you, for constant heart." Here "none" has a strictly human reference, denoting "'nobody else.'" Such a heart distinguishes the friend both from inconstant Helen and from Adonis, who might be termed "nonconstant" for declining the commitment to love that fidelity presupposes.

The "constant heart" that terminates Sonnet 53 anticipates 54, which begins:

> Oh how much more doth beauty beauteous seem
> By that sweet ornament which truth doth give.

—Joseph Pequigney, *Such Is My Love: A Study of Shakespeare's Sonnets.* (Chicago: University of Chicago Press, 1985), pp. 53–55. ☯

JONATHAN BATE ON SHAKESPEARE'S INNOVATION IN SONNET 53

[Jonathan Bate is King Alfred Professor of English Literature at the University of Liverpool. His books include *Shakespeare and the English Romantic Imagination* (1989) and *Shakespeare and Ovid* (1993).]

In Barnes the Ovidian mythological figures are fixed points, ideal substances which are shadowed in his own love. In Shakespeare the opposite is the case: the lovely boy is t he substance, the mythological figure the shadow. 'Describe Adonis, and the counterfeit / Is poorly imitated after you': where Barnes offers counterfeits, poor imitations of Ovidian originals, Shakespeare makes the lovely boy into the ideal figure of beauty and Adonis into the counterfeit. The third quatrain performs a similar trumping, in this instance an overgoing of those figures of natural plenty who are so central to Ovid's world: 'Speak of the spring and foison of the year', and one would usually speak of Proserpina and Ceres, but here nature is a shadow of the youth's beauty. The sonnet's innovation is in its appropriation of the term 'imitate'. Where a poet like Giles Fletcher announces on the title-page of his sonnet-sequence *Licia* (1593) that he is writing in 'imitation of the best Latin Poets, and others', Shakespeare claims within his poem that classical figures are imitations of his own beloved. 'Figure' is an analogous term: *paradigma* is a figure of speech whereby classical figures serve as authorities, but Sonnet 106 goes so far as to make the claim that all praises of past beauties 'are but prophecies / Of this our time, all you prefiguring'. The ideal figures are but prefigurings of the poet's present love.

When Shakespeare deploys this effect of inverted *paradigma*, he exercises a turn on the concept of metamorphosis. The paradigmatic function of myth is to provide poet and reader with a stock of archetypes. But where it is customary to suggest the force of a present change by comparing it to traditional mythological metamorphosis that is known to be forceful, Shakespeare makes the myths into the shadow, the present change into the archetype or true substance. In Ovid, extreme emotion precipitates the metamorphosis of a person into an object of nature, whereas in Sonnet 113, extreme emotion precipitates the metamorphosis of the objects of nature into a person:

> [Mine eye] no form delivers to the heart
> Of bird, of flower, or shape which it doth latch.
> Of his quick objects hath the mind no part,
> Nor his own vision holds what it doth catch;
> For if it see the rud'st of gentlest sight,
> The most sweet favored or deformèd'st creature,
> The mountain or the sea, the day or night,
> The crow or dove, it shapes them to your feature.

The sympathetic eye of Ovid looks at the natural world and reads out of it an array of mythic lovers and objects of desire; the possessed eye/I of the Sonnets sees in all forms of nature its own love, its single object of desire.

But Shakespeare does not always seem so readily able to overturn his prototypes. Sonnet 59 opens with a troubled expression of poetic belatedness:

If there be nothing new, but that which is
Hath been before, how are our brains beguiled,
Which, labouring for invention, bear amiss
The second burden of a former child!

The darkness of this is manifest if we recollect Holofernes' distinction between *imitari*, which is nothing, and 'the jerks of invention' to which the poet should aspire. Whereas Shakespeare proved his inventiveness in Sonnet 53 by appropriating the idea of imitation, now he laments that the labour for originality is fruitless since nothing is new, what one writes will already be written, and what one imagines to be the child of one's invention will turn out to be the child of one's poetic father.

—Jonathan Bate, *Shakespeare and Ovid.* (Oxford: Oxford University Press, 1993), pp. 89–90.

(৩)

Sonnet 55

G. WILSON KNIGHT ON SONNET 55 AND THE POWER OF POETRY

[G. Wilson Knight (1897–1939), a leading British Shakespeare scholar, taught drama and English literature at the University of Leeds. He was the author of many volumes of criticism, including *The Wheel of Fire* (1930), *The Starlit Dome* (1941), *The Crown of Life* (1947), and *Shakespeare and Religion* (1967). This extract was taken from his book *The Mutual Flame* (1955). Knight approaches the Sonnets as the spiritual underpinning of all Shakespeare's work. For him, the Sonnets deal with issues of time, death, and eternity in the context of sexual drive and their bisexual nature is a window to Shakespeare's dramas.]

See how clear is the thought in the final couplet: the young man's immortality is not questioned. He will rise, presumably in good repair, at the day of judgment. But if so, what is all the fuss about? What does it matter whether he be known to readers of poetry during the few intervening centuries?

Clearly, there is more in the sonnet than this. It is throughout filled to overflowing with the elixir, the ecstasy, the dithyrambic certainties. Observe that the main emphasis is on, not love, but the powers of poetry. We have already seen how poetry is in the Sonnets felt as a medium for supernal intuitions. Here every image piles up to suggest that the poetry enjoys an authority, or exists from a dimension, to which all temporal fabrications and engagements are as nothing; and the weightiest and most serious are chosen for the purpose. This poetic authority creates a 'living record'. The phrase recalls the living God of the Gospels and St. Paul; like that god, it is a conqueror over death. Read so, there need be no worry about the incompatibility introduced by 'doom' and 'judgment' day, since a context has been generated of sufficient power to absorb them with all their awful associations, into the main assertion. The two ways of eternal understanding, religion and poetry, are happily balanced in our final juxtaposition of 'judgment' and 'lovers' eyes'.

—G. Wilson Knight, *The Mutual Flame*. (London: Meuthen & Co. Ltd., 1955), p. 100.

LOWRY NELSON JR. ON RHYME IN THE SONNETS

[Lowry Nelson Jr., late Professor of Comparative Literature at Yale University, is the author of *Baroque Lyric Poetry* (1961) and "The Fictive Reader and Literary Self-reflexiveness."]

In Sonnet 55 there is a finer use that is even flaunted by the two contrasting pairs, masonry/memory and enmity/posterity, which have the *force* of riming in two syllables. On rare occasions Shakespeare rimes inexactly, as in field/held, fleet'st/sweets, o'erread/dead, and open/broken. But almost always, even in the poor sonnets (of which there are too many for a great poet), the rimes are good and serviceable, as rime in the main ought to be.

As a conscientious poet Shakespeare had the conviction of his rimes, and in some clear cases was put to shifts to make the sense and rhythm come out at least acceptably. A common fault in rimed poetry—which Shakespeare in his best sonnets worked to avoid—is, as I have noted, the lame relative clause or descriptive phrase that could better have been a single word. It is, of course, difficult to distinguish padding from convincing colloquial prolixity; besides, extreme compression can well be a fault, as it is in quite a few of Shakespeare's sonnets that have to many seemed obscure. In this regard it is interesting to compare Sonnets 55 and 116, the first in the *exegi monumentum* vein, the second on the constancy of love. In 55 we read, as the poem exaltedly and rather verbosedly flows,

> . . . your praise shall still find room
> Even in the eyes of all posterity
> That wear this world out to the ending doom.

The rime and the notion are accommodated. Yet the last line given here seems rhythmically weak and too long as an enjambed descriptive clause, lamely and otiosely modifying "doom" with "ending." In 116, which begins less strikingly, we find "doom" (which I take to be a true rime here in Shakespeare's pronunciation) again in the same position at the end of the twelfth line:

> Love's not Time's fool, though rosy lips and cheeks
> Within his bending sickle's compass come;
> Love alters not with his brief hours and weeks,
> But bears it out even to the edge of doom.

Here, to begin with, the clause is independent and the verb-phrase "bears it out" is not weakened by a long object ("it" vs. "this world"). The trochaic stress on "even" tilts the line toward a strong conclusion with two climactic stresses on "edge" and "doom." Thus the word "doom," resonant in both sound and sense, can express its full and elemental import. Incidentally the rhythmic force, to my ear, shortens "even" to "evn." These two passages are clearly related, not so much in subject matter or sense as in sound and technique. We are in Shakespeare's ear.

Such experiments in sound, and more particularly in the potency of rime words in different contexts, are naturally part of a poet's activity. Other instances could be adduced—for example, the rime hope/scope in sonnets 52 and 29: in the first it is used in the concluding couplet with the then ordinary meaning of "scope" as "purpose" or "means"; in the second ("Desiring this man's art and that man's scope") these forceful words are separated in the second quatrain and "scope" takes on what was then a new meaning of "range." There are numerous other instances in which it could be argued that Shakespeare might have been thinking in rime-pairs and testing them out. One must, however, be wary and aware that some of his best sonnets show no remarkable inventiveness in rime and that some of his virtuoso rimes (as well as wordplay and conceits) occur in faulty and lightweight poems.

> —Lowry Nelson Jr. "The Matter of Rime: Sonnets of Sidney, Daniel, and Shakespeare." In *Poetic Traditions of the English Renaissance*, ed. Maynard Mack and George deForest Lord. (New Haven, CT: Yale University Press, 1982), pp. 135–136.

HOWARD FELPERIN ON SHAKESPEARE'S RHETORICAL STRATEGY IN SONNET 55

[Howard Felperin is the Robert Wallace Professor of English at Melbourne University in Australia. His books include *Shakespearean Romance* (1972), *Shakespearean Representation* (1977), and *Beyond Deconstruction: The Uses and Abuses of Literary Theory* (1985).]

In pointing to the rhetorical nature of Shakespeare's enunciation of poetic authority and perdurability in 55, I am not suggesting that its force can wholly be explained in terms of a renaissance rhetorical programme then in place, or that adherence to such a programme is what insures its poetic success. In fact, Shakespeare's poem, with its initial restatement and subsequent elaboration of a Horatian and Ovidian *topos*, does illustrate a principle fundamental to renaissance rhetorical theory, namely that of *copia*, of virtuoso elaboration on a received theme. This widespread rhetorical practice may well be regarded as the renaissance counterpart or forerunner of the postromantic phenomenon of creative misprision, a means of engaging and overgoing classical models and thereby extending a potentially tongue-tying tradition by reweaving it.

Such commonplace rhetorical tactics as hyperbole and negative comparison, both employed in the opening line of 55, are in the service of this larger rhetorical strategy. The frequent and characteristic recourse to hyperbole, often combined with classical allusion, is familiar enough as a chief constituent of Marlowe's mighty line, from which Shakespeare doubtless learned much, and negative comparison is one of the chief means by which Milton aspires to overgo classical epic, 'to soar above th'Aonian mount': '*Not* that fair field of Enna. . .' The extravagant variation on a received topic characterizes Shakespeare's own earliest efforts in epyllion, comedy, and tragedy; his *Venus and Adonis* and *Rape of Lucrece* multiply the metamorphoses of their Ovidian sources, and his *Comedy of Errors* and *Titus Andronicus,* the mistaken identities and vindictive atrocities of Plautus' *Menaechmi* and Seneca's *Thyestes* respectively. This rhetorical gambit is no doubt also at work in the bold paradoxes with which he develops the traditional poetic claims of Horatian and Ovidian sources in 55, so as to revivify and redouble their old force through the surcharge of a new rhetorical *energia*.

It would be grossly reductive, however, to think that 55—or the *Sonnets* generally, since this is their persistent undertheme—authorize themselves simply through single-minded following out of a renaissance rhetorical programme. After all, the strategy of *copia,* with its panoply of particular rhetorical tactics, is itself only a norm or model that by its own logic would itself have to be exceeded for a true authority to emerge. Great numbers of Elizabethan sonnets, including that of Spenser/du Bellay, make some of the same moves as Shakespeare's 55 in rhetorically invoking and extending classical precedent to legitimate themselves, yet fail to make good their poetic aspirations in the only way they can be made good: by compelling future readings. Shakespeare himself complains half way through his sequence that the imitation of his own rhetoric by rival poets has left him barren and tongue-tied, 'enforced to seek anew / Some fresher stamp of the time-bett'ring days.' To achieve the kind of poetic authority Shakespeare envisions, he would have to tap some 'source' deeper and more powerful than any set of classical examples or programme of rhetorical variation, thereby anticipating and pre-empting his own potential imitation and obsolescence at the hands of others. His poetry would have to be different from its own potential rhetorical reduction or anatomization.

This does not mean that the authority Shakespeare envisions and claims has nothing to do with rhetoric, only that it is not rhetorical in any simple sense, i.e. that it is not logical, or has empirical designs on its putative objects and potential readers, or uses a repertory of devices for effecting those designs. The project so confidently proclaimed in 55 seems closer to the rhetorical mode described by Paul de Man and Roland Barthes, as 'performative'. Barthes defines a 'performative' utterance, adopting the term from J. L. Austin, as 'a rare verbal form (exclusively given in the first person and in the present tense) in which the enunciation has no other content (contains no other proposition) than the act by which it is uttered — something like the *I declare* of kings or the *I sing* of very ancient poets.

Though not exactly cast in present tense, and without giving up all empirical designs on its object and audience, Sonnet 55 seems very close to this performative mode in its aspiration to a royal or bardic bringing into being of its object, to making itself good and itself flesh in something like the eternal present of its utterance. So it might well seem tempting at this point to try to account for the triumphant poetic authority of Sonnet 55—as opposed to the more limited authority of any of a number of its Elizabethan congeners—as a function of this performative quality, that is, in terms of the consistency and integrity with which it maintains the self-subsistence of its performative mode.

—Howard Felperin, *Beyond Deconstruction: The Uses and Abuses of Literary Theory*. (Oxford: Clarendon Press, 1985), pp. 159–161.

⊕

ANTHONY HECHT ON THE CLASSICAL ROOTS OF SONNET 55

[Anthony Hecht is a poet who was born in 1923 in New York City. He retired in 1993 after 40 years of teaching at Bard College, Kenyon College, Smith College, the University of Rochester, Iowa State University, and Georgetown University. His books include *The Collected, Earlier Poetry of Anthony Hecht* and *The Transparent Man*. His latest publications are a collection of poems, *Flight Among the Tombs* (1996) and the Introduction to the New Cambridge Shakespeare edition of the Sonnets (1996).]

It needs immediately to be said that this is not personal vanity, nor even a shrewd intuition on Shakespeare's part, but a poetic convention that can be traced back to classical antiquity. It can be found in Homer and Virgil, and J. B. Leishman noted that 'passages on the immortalizing power of poetry are very frequent in the Pindar's Odes'. This tradition was so strong among the Pléiade—the group of poets who acclimatised the sonnet form in France—that Ronsard in one of his sonnets threatened to withhold immortality from one particular unnamed lady unless she acceded to his decidedly carnal desire. The convention is to be found in Spenser's 'Epithalamion':

> Song made in lieu of many ornaments,
> With which my love should duly have bene dect...
> Be unto her a goodly ornament,
> And for short time an endlesse moniment

and in Shakespeare's own Sonnet 55:

> Not marble nor the gilded monuments
> Of princes shall outlive this pow'rful rhyme.

If Shakespeare is undoubtedly invoking an ancient convention in asserting the poet's capacity to confer immortality, it is not the only convention he employs in his sonnets. We commonly assume that, whatever else love may be, it is at the very least a spontaneous and undeniable impulse, but it was not always thought to be so, and in the Renaissance, views about it were much more complicated. One modern critic has declared flatly: 'L'amour? une invention du douziéme siécle.' What could seem more pedantically offensive to our habits of feeling and thought? But the fact is that in classical literature, love is almost invariably regarded as an aberration, a dangerous taking leave of one's senses, most likely to lead to catastrophe and generally to be deplored. Many of the greatest Greek tragedies—*Oedipus Rex, Medea, Hippolytus, The Bacchae*—treat love as a tragic madness; so does Virgil in the episode of Dido in the *Aeneid.* The whole calamity of the Trojan war was brought about by a surrender to this insane impulse, which is treated in the Iliad as altogether unworthy and trifling in comparison with grave matters of war and heroism. The hero Odysseus, in the *Odyssey,* rejects all manner of solicitations from Calypso, Circe, and the Sirens; all these kinds of love are dangerous and to be avoided. Romantic love was historically a late development, and first manifested itself in Provence during the age of medieval feudalism, to which it bears a kind of metaphorical resemblance.

In the poetry developed by the troubadours and poets of Languedoc, the poet-lover always humbles himself in a submissive relationship to his beloved, a posture that duplicates the relation of a vassal towards his feudal lord. Indeed, as C. S. Lewis has pointed out, the lover addresses his beloved as *midons,* 'which etymologically represents not "my lady" but "my lord"'. Lewis notes that 'The lover is always abject. Obedience to his lady's lightest wish, however whimsical, and silent acquiescence in her rebukes, however unjust, are the only virtues he dares to claim.' He goes on to assert that 'an unmistakable continuity connects the Provençal love song with the love poetry of the later Middle Ages, and thence, through Petrarch and many others, with that of the present day'. Anyone reading Shakespeare's Sonnet 57—'Being your slave, what should I do but tend / Upon the hours and times of your desire?'—would do well to remember the strength and antiquity of this tradition. It is a tradition virtually insisted on in the final couplet of that sonnet:

> So true a fool is love that in your will
> (Though you do any thing) he thinks no ill.

This is more than merely abject; 'true' in these lines means not only genuinely and certifiably a fool but also 'faithful'. The implication is that folly not merely exposes one to folly but requires it.

These matters of tradition and convention lead us directly to the insoluble question of just what in the Sonnets may be said to be (as Wordsworth claimed they were) a key with which Shakespeare unlocked his heart, and what may instead be attributed to a traditional posture belonging to the fourteen-line love poem that he inherited. Are we to regard these poems as anything other than the surviving pages of an intimate diary, transcribing the poet's exact and authentic feelings on every topic he addresses? There are always readers who seek, not art, but something documentary and unassailably factual; when these two categories seem mysteriously intermingled, they will always prize the second over the first.

> —Anthony Hecht, Introduction to "The Sonnets." *SC Yearbook 1996*
> 37, p. 351.

Sonnet 87

Murray Krieger on the Poet's Punctured Dream

[Murray Krieger was Professor of English at the University of California in Los Angeles until 1982. He is the author of *The Tragic Vision: Variations on a Theme in Literary Interpretation* (1960), *The Play and Place of Criticism* (1967), *The Classic Vision: The Retreat from Extremity in Modern Literature* (1971), and *Poetic Presence and Illusion: Essays in Critical History and Theory*. He is also the author of *A Window to Criticism: Shakespeare's Sonnets and Modern Poetics* (1964), from which this extract is taken. Krieger suggests that Shakespeare's Sonnets comprise a "memorial tomb of love to which, as a womb, it gives eternal life" (193). He finds in the Sonnets a key to the nature of poetry and poetics, and he focuses on their mirror-window metaphorical system.]

Perhaps our definitive word on the promises and deceptions of truth should be spoken by Sonnet 87, which turns out to be a non-Petrarchan commentary on the Petrarchan lover's lowliness.

> Farewell! thou art too dear for my possessing,
> And like enough thou know'st thy estimate.
> The charter of thy worth gives thee releasing;
> My bonds in thee are all determinate.
> For how do I hold thee but by thy granting,
> And for that riches where is my deserving?
> The cause of this fair gift in me is wanting,
> And so my patent back again is swerving.
> Thyself thou gav'st, thy own worth then not knowing,
> Or me, to whom thou gav'st it, else mistaking:
> So great thy gift, upon misprision growing,
> Comes home again, on better judgment making.
> > Thus I have had thee as a dream doth flatter—
> > In sleep a king, but waking no such matter.

Here the marketplace tone and the marketplace reasoning are so insistent as to be unmistakable—and resented. The pun on "dear" in the first line, for all its obviousness, still manages to be effective because, in bringing together one meaning from the world of sentiment and one meaning from the marketplace, it sends forth the two poles that create both the dialectic and the unity of the poem—indeed of all these poems, singly and as a group. When we first read "dear," we assume that it functions in the Petrarchan context of affections (despite "possessing"), only in retrospect to be shocked by the word "estimate" and all that follows into recognizing that we have been taken in, have been sentimental fools insufficiently aware of how the world really operates and, consequently, of how the word "dear" must really operate. The unbroken multiplication of legal and financial terms throughout the octave shouts almost too loudly the poet's bitterness at having the one kind of "dear" reduced to the other, at having love's world of troth reduced to the niggardly world of truth, the world of faith to the world of fact. He uses his metric to this end also, with a maddening inexorability. The almost unvarying use of the feminine ending bestows a sing-song matter-of-factness to each line, each end-stopped with the voice dropped. No counter-statement is possible: the figures speak for themselves. Only lines 2 and 4 in the poem do not have feminine endings, and even in these the extremely weak final foot ("estimate," "determinate") gives much the same effect. Except for the couplet, the other lines all end in the "ing," either in participle or gerund. And the couplet, despite the shift, has its own feminine ending. . . .

So the poet has been flattered by both the friend and the dream, while the awakening deprives him of both:

> Thus I have had thee as a dream doth flatter—
> In sleep a king, but waking no such matter.

The couplet barely hints at the conjunction of king, flattery, and golden illusion, which is more fully developed elsewhere. . . . Here, as in other cases we have seen where explication is enriched by considering the *Sonnets* as a single body of metaphor, I believe we may borrow from the complete development of an image cluster in one sonnet to fill out the mere allusion to it elsewhere. The lowly poet, in being flattered by the delusive dream of love, was converted into a king. As in Sonnet 114, his faithful mind had as its subjects the obedient senses which allowed themselves to be asleep to truth in the flattering service of troth. Now is the rude awakening, as truth— which is here restricted to proper calculation—asserts itself. The awakening is poetically rude too: after the idyllic reminiscence of line 13 and the first two feet of line 14, there is a sharp letdown in the last three feet. First, "In sleep a king," but then a total break aided by the caesura, and finally "but waking no such matter": the total dismissal of everything as the punctured dream with the omnibus prosaism, "no such matter." Is it too much to see the last word, the casually and vaguely uttered "matter," as taking on a precision and becoming something of a pun, since it has resulted from the intrusion of the world of "matter," the materialistic world of the marketplace, upon the fond, more-than-marketplace dream—the dream of a world of faith in which worth is not all, or at least is not to be measured by marketplace values? And is this not another form of Shakespeare's judgment on the unmagical, unyielding mirror, measure of the measurable world that, in its vile wisdom, dares not extend itself? Is it not also his mixed judgment on the wormy modern world with its necessary truths, the late, post-chivalric, pragmatic world that we recognize as the world of that mixed hero, Bolingbroke?

The mention of Bolingbroke may lead us to the possibility that it is rather the beloved of Sonnet 87 who has been the king and who, in the couplet, is deprived of his kingliness by the poet's awakening. The syntax of the couplet would perhaps seem to support this even more bitter reading rather than the earlier one. I have had thee as a dream doth flatter: I have had thee in sleep as a king, but on waking I find you to be no such matter. In succumbing to the table of equivalents, the values of the marketplace, the friend has lowered himself from the glory he shared with the poet when, despite his greater worth, he accepted with the poet their common dream of faith. According to love's paradoxical propriety, in accepting the egalitarianism of love he was truly regal; in now accepting the marketplace estimate of his greater worth, he is "no such matter." Indeed, may it not be the beloved friend who has suffered the greater fall? And the final word of that final phrase that seems to have been tossed out carelessly, "matter," as material, has all the force and more that I suggested in my earlier reading. For the friend's "matter" has been transformed by the end of the dream and the mutual awakening to marketplace reality, with the mutual revaluation that it imposes. The "stuff" that "dreams are made on" has no more stability than the dreams themselves.

—Murray Krieger, *A Window to Criticism.* (Princeton, NJ: Princeton University Press, 1964), pp. 133–137.

JOSEPH PEQUIGNEY ON THE ROLE OF PHYSICAL PASSION IN SONNET 87

[Joseph Pequigney is Professor of English at the State University of New York at Stony Brook. In his book *Such Is My Love: A Study of Shakespeare's Sonnets,* from which this extract is taken, Pequigney argues that the sonnet sequence represents "the grand masterpiece of homoerotic poetry." He describes a complex and psychologically realistic story of the poet's erotic attachment to the fair young man of Sonnets 1–126. Sonnets 127–154, dealing with the dark lady, are read as a footnote to the jealousy crisis described in sonnets 40–42. The first 126 sonnets depict a sexual relationship between the poet and the youth that complies with Freud's views on homosexuality.]

To look on past joys and to feel like a king when contented are common enough notions, and these verses include them but say more. Shakespeare realizes, with Freud, that dreams "flatter" in being wish-fulfillments; to be "in sleep a king" is to command whatever the sleeper's heart desires; and the dream material, or "matter," is conceived of as libidinal in character, for what is dreamt of is of having "had thee" in the erotic sense of the verb. The dream psychology here has a figurative status, being incorporated into a simile meant to convey the poet's impression that, once "waking" to the current reality of the youth's unavailability, the memories of sexual fruition with him take on a dreamlike aura.

The bawdy wordplay in Sonnet 87, no more restricted to the couplet than that of 52, is introduced at the very outset: "Farewell, thou art too dear for my [carnal] possessing." This gerund carries the same idea as "had" in 87.13. In between, at 87.9, appears the clause "Thy self thou gav'st," and Partridge and Coleman agree that 'giving oneself' in Shakespeare can = 'sexual yielding.' In this setting, 87.5, "For how do I hold thee but by thy granting," admits of the reading, 'I take you in my arms only with your consent.'

Sonnet 87 has a formal affinity with Sonnet 20, whose rhymes also are all feminine, and with Sonnet 52 it has affinities of diction, which include the word "worth," used twice in both, in Sonnet 87 at lines 3 and 9 to signify 'value' or 'excellence' based on personal beauty. Allusions to beauty occur also in "that riches," "this fair gife," and "thy great gift" (87.6, 7, and 11), where the gift is that of the comely body was that amorously granted out of an underestimation of yourself ("thy own worth then not knowing") or your overestimation of myself ("where is my deserving?").

Why the self-abasement? Shakespeare could hardly be unaware of his superlative genius, and, to leave the question of autobiography aside, the fictive persona shows himself elsewhere to be fully confident of his capacity to compose undying verse. Class differences cannot be the answer, unless one is prepared to argue that the friend remained unaware of his noble rank until *after* he had yielded himself in love. The poet's self-depreciation, rather, issues from the same source as his awe: from the passionate response to the youth's exceptional good looks on the part of the older man, who feels himself deficient precisely in the physical qualities that elicit his desire. Once the beloved realizes how rare his attractiveness is, can he remain satisfied with such a lover? The lover who fears rejection anticipates and even justifies it, though surely he does so in the hope of forestalling it.

—Joseph Pequigney, *Such Is My Love.* (Chicago: University of Chicago Press, 1985), pp. 46, 49.

⚭

JOHNATHAN BATE ON READING BEYOND THE TEXT OF SONNET 87

[Jonathan Bate is King Alfred Professor of English Literature at the University of Liverpool. His books include *Shakespeare and the English Romantic Imagination* (1989) and *Shakespeare and Ovid* (1993), from which this extract is taken.]

The real melancholy of the sequence comes from the way in which the poet is *impressed*, not by Ovid, not by the 'rival poet', but by the fair youth himself. The sense in which Ovid, and indeed the whole panegyric tradition, begets the sonnets is less troubling than that in which the youth himself begets them and can reject them. . . . [Sonnet 87] is troubled not about the poetic tradition but about the whims of the beloved. Like Hermia's father, the youth has the power to mould another person's self; he is able to shape the poet, "To leave the figure or disfigure it". Anxiety is wrought by the fear of losing the beloved; the truly terrifying thought is that he has only been possessed in a dream. Images of literary textuality are replaced by those of legal and commercial textuality. The instability of both desire and patronage are central concerns here. The speaker of the sonnet shares Actaeon's discovery that the person you desire has the greatest power to destroy you. The 'swerving' is not between the text and its aesthetic paradigm, but of the 'patent' back to the 'I' who has registered it; the 'misprision' is of the 'gift' of love which in this poem sounds suspiciously like a cipher for that of patronage. If the sonnet is to be granted its force, extra-textual reality must be allowed to intrude in some such terms as these.

> —Jonathan Bate, *Shakespeare and Ovid.* (New York: Oxford University Press, 1993), p. 97.

ⓒ

Anthony Hecht on the Question of Blame in Sonnet 87

[Anthony Hecht is a poet who was born in 1923 in New York City. He retired in 1993 after 40 years of teaching at Bard College, Kenyon College, Smith College, the University of Rochester, Iowa State University, and Georgetown University. His books include *The Collected, Earlier Poetry of Anthony Hecht* and *The Transparent Man.* His latest publications are a collection of poems, *Flight Among the Tombs* (1996) and the Introduction to the New Cambridge Shakespeare edition of the Sonnets (1996).]

The genius of this poem consists in its absolute command of total complexity throughout, by which it is left brilliantly ambiguous—through tact and diplomacy, with bitterness and irony, or with matter-of-fact worldliness—just which of the two parties involved is to be blamed for the impasse and end of what had once been a deeply binding relationship. The pretext of the poem is one of self-mortification characteristic of the traditional early love sonnets. . . . The lover insists upon his own unworthiness, particularly as regards the exalted, unapproachable condition of the beloved. Although there is a pun on the word 'dear' in the first line—a pun made more explicit by the possibly commercial language of the second line— puns are not the building blocks of this poem as they are of others. The lover begins in what seems initially to be a spirit of generous renunciation: the line can mean both (1) 'I am prepared to give you up' and (2) 'I appear not to have much choice in the matter, so I am giving you up.' Taken in conjunction with the first line, however, the second line in the poem seems to include or suggest the following possible meanings:

(1) You know how much I love you.
(2) You know how much you deserve to be loved.
(3) You have a very high opinion of yourself.
(4) You know how much others love you.
(5) You know the value of the opinions of
    (a) me
    (b) yourself
    (c) others
    (d) all of us.

The poem continues to manoeuvre between these modes of worldliness and unworldliness in a way that, by its skill, speaks of two different kinds of pain, and at the same time makes the pain almost tolerable by the sheer act of lively intelligence that went into the making of the poem, which is clearly no raw, unmediated transcription of experience. By the time we reach the end of the second line, the poem has begun to seethe with implied hostility, governed nevertheless by conventions of propriety and the decorum of charity. We cannot fail to notice the persuasive language of law and commerce, those two ledger-keeping modes of coming to terms with the world; and we cannot fail to feel the irony of the application of those modes to questions of love.

The speaker here seems to be giving the beloved a writ of freedom to depart, and justifying that departure by several different kinds of 'reason', generally practical and intended as plausible. The words 'estimate', 'charter', 'bonds', 'riches', 'gift', 'patent', 'misprision', and 'judgment' all speak, as might a shrewd auctioneer, from a market-place perspective. Beneath the surface of supposedly self-abnegating relinquishment, we detect a flavour of bitterness and scarcely repressed resentment. This may be most openly expressed, and at the same time best concealed, by the lines

> For how do I hold thee but by thy granting,
> And for that riches where is my deserving?

We do not love anyone on the basis of merit, or rank, or wealth, or for other worldly advantages. Love mixed with or tainted by calculation is highly suspect—is indeed not love at all. It follows then that if the beloved is willing to accept as a legitimate excuse for withdrawing from the relationship any of the 'worldly' and practical excuses proposed by the lover, then the lover cannot but conclude that the love has not been mutual, whatever he may have thought it to begin with; that the beloved, surveying the prospect or prospects, has both reason and right to seek elsewhere, since no real love seems to be involved. The very word 'misprision' means both a misunderstanding or mistake, and also a clerical error of the ledger-keeping sort. The final irony of the poem lies in the fact that both parties were deeply deceived — the beloved by either underestimating himself or overestimating the lover, and the lover by having believed that he was loved.

> —Anthony Hecht, Introduction to "The Sonnets." *SC Yearbook 1996* 37, pp. 356–357.

HAROLD BLOOM ON THE MEANING OF "MISPRISION" IN SONNET 87

[Harold Bloom is Sterling Professor of the Humanities at Yale University and Berg Professor of English at New York University. He is the author of more than 20 books, including the best-selling *The Western Canon* (1994) and *The Book of J* (1990), and is the editor of over 400 anthologies of both literature and literary criticism. His works include *Shelley's Mythmaking* (1959), *Blake's Apocalypse* (1963), *Yeats* (1970), *A Map of Misreading* (1975), *Kab-*

balah and Criticism (1975), *Wallace Stevens: The Poems of Our Climate* (1977), *Agon: Towards a Theory of Revisionism* (1982), *American Religion* (1992), and *Omens of Millennium*(1996). *The Anxiety of Influence* (1973), from which this extract is taken, sets forth Bloom's theory of the literary relationships between great writers and their predecessors.]

"Swerving" and "misprision" both depend upon "mistaking" as an ironical over-esteeming or over-estimation, here in Sonnet 87. Whether Shakespeare ruefully is lamenting, with a certain reserve, the loss of the Earl of Southampton as a lover, or as a friend, is not (fortunately) a matter upon which certitude is possible. Palpably and profoundly an erotic poem, Sonnet 87 (not by design) can also be read as an allegory of any writer's (or person's) relation to tradition, particularly as embodied in a figure taken as one's own forerunner. The speaker of Sonnet 87 is aware that he had been made an offer that he could not refuse, which is a dark insight into the nature of authentic tradition. "Misprision" for Shakespeare, as opposed to "mistaking," implied not only misunderstanding or misreading but tended also to be a punning word-play suggesting unjust imprisonment. Perhaps "misprision" in Shakespeare also means a scornful underestimation: either way, he took the legal term and gave it an aura of deliberate or willful misinterpretation. "Swerving," in Sonnet 87, is only secondarily a returning; primarily it indicates an unhappy freedom.

—Harold Bloom, "The Anguish of Contamination." Preface to *The Anxiety of Influence.* 2nd ed. (New York and Oxford: Oxford University Press, 1997), pp. xi–xiii.

Sonnet 94

SIR WILLIAM EMPSON ON THE USE OF FLATTERY IN SONNET 94

[Sir William Empson (1906–1984) was a British poet and critic known for his immense influence on 20th-century literary criticism and for his metaphysical poetry. *Seven Types of Ambiguity* (1930) is essentially a close examination of poetic texts. He applied his critical method to longer texts in *Some Versions of Pastoral* (1935), from which this extract is taken, and in *The Structure of Complex Words* (1951). He taught English literature at the University of Tokyo, Peking National University of China, and at Sheffield University.]

But the machinery of the statement is peculiar; its clash of admiration and contempt seems dependent on a clash of feeling about the classes. One might connect it with that curious trick of pastoral which for extreme courtly flattery—perhaps to give self-respect to both poet and patron, to show that the poet is not ignorantly easy to impress, nor the patron to flatter—writes about the poorest people; and with those jazz songs which give an intense effect of luxury and silk underwear by pretending to be about slaves naked in the fields. To those who care chiefly about biography this trick must seem monstrously tantalising; Wilde built the paradox of his essay on it, and it is true that Shakespeare might have set the whole thing to work from the other end about a highly trained mudlark brought in to act his princesses. But it is the very queerness of the trick that makes it so often useful in building models of the human mind; and yet the power no less than the universality of this poem depends on generalising the trick so completely as to seem independent of it.

> But if that flowre with base infection meete,
> The basest weed out-braues his dignity:
>> For sweetest things turn sowrest by their deedes,
>> Lilies that fester, smell far worse than weeds.

It is not clear how the metaphor from 'meet' acts; it may be like 'meet with disaster'—'if it catches infection, which would be bad luck,' or like meeting someone in the street, as most men do safely—'*any* contact with infection is fatal to so peculiarly placed a creature.' The first applies to the natural and unprotected flower, the second to the lily that has the hubris and fate of greatness. They are not of course firmly separated, but lilies are separated from *flower* by a colon and an intervening generalisation, whereas the flower is only separated from the cold people (not all of whom need be lilies) by a colon; certainly the flower as well as the lily is in danger, but this does not make them identical and equal to W. H. The neighboring sonnets continually say that his deeds can do nothing to destroy his sweetness, and this seems to make the terrible last line point at him somewhat less directly. One may indeed take it as 'Though so debauched, you keep your looks. Only mean people who never give themselves heartily to anything can do that. But the best hypocrite is found out in the end, and shown as the worst.' But Shakespeare may also be congratulating W. H. on an imperfection which acts as a preservative; he is a son of the world and can protect himself, like the cold people, or a spontaneous and therefore fresh sinner, like the flower; he may safely stain, as heaven's sun, the kisser of carrion, staineth. At any rate it is not of virginity, at this stage, that he can be accused. The smell of a big lily is so lush and insolent, suggests so powerfully both incense and pampered flesh—the traditional metaphor about it is perfect—that its festering can only be that due to the hubris of spirituality; it is ironically generous to apply it to the careerist to whom hypocrisy is recommended; and yet in the fact that we seem to apply it to him there is a glance backwards, as if to justify him, at the ambition involved in even the most genuine attempt on heaven. You may say that Shakespeare dragged in the last line as a quotation from *Edward III* that doesn't quite fit; it is also possible that (as often happens to poets, who tend to make in their lives a situation they have already written about) he did not till now see the full width of its application.

In a sense the total effect is an evasion of Shakespeare's problem; it gives him a way of praising W. H. in spite of anything. In the flower the oppositions are transcended; it is because it is self-concentrated that it has so much more to give and because it is undesigning that it is more grandiose in beauty than Solomon. But it is held in mind chiefly for comfort; none of the people suggested to us are able to imitate it very successfully; nor if they could would they be safe. Yet if W. H. has festered, that at least makes him a lily, and at least not a stone; if he is not a lily, he is in the less danger of festering.

I must try to sum up the effect of so complex an irony, half by trying to follow it through a gradation. 'I am praising to you the contemptible things you admire, you little plotter; this is how the others try to betray you through flattery; yet it is your little generosity, though it show only as lewdness, which will betray you; for it is wise to be cold, both because you are too inflammable and because I have been so much hurt by you who are heartless; yet I can the better forgive you through that argument from our common isolation; I must praise to you your very faults, especially your selfishness, because you can only now be safe by cultivating them further; yet this is the most dangerous of necessities; people are greedy for your fall as for that of any of the great; indeed no one can rise above common life, as you have done so fully, without in the same degree sinking below it; you have made this advice real to me, because I cannot despise it for your sake; I am only sure that you are valuable and in danger.'

—William Empson, *Some Versions of Pastoral.* (Norfolk, CT: New Directions, 1935), pp. 98–101.

☙

EDWARD HUBLER ON THE FAMILIAR IMAGERY IN SONNET 94

[Edward Hubler taught at the University of Rochester in New York and Princeton University. He is the author of *The Sense of Shakespeare's Sonnets* (1952) and the editor of *The Riddle of Shakespeare's Sonnets* (1962). Hubler observes that the sonnet provided a means of expression for Shakespeare's major ideas before he was able to represent them in the medium of drama: the perception of friendship, the dynamics of personality, the power of love and lust. He offers a thematic approach to the Sonnets.]

Everything about the poem invites comment, from the private force of the opening phrases to the last line, which, one editor assures us, "is not true." The recorded conjectures about it are rich in everything that conjecture can lead to, and in recent years it has been the object of more critical analyses than any other sonnet. If we approach it in the light of Shakespeare's other works, we might find it less difficult than it appears.

A survey of Shakespeare's works will show that this sonnet employs his most familiar imagery and that the thought of the sonnet, bit by bit, is to be found everywhere. Primarily it is the articulation of the parts which puzzles. On first reading the sonnet, we shall, of course, notice the irony of the first eight lines; and everything that we find in the other works will confirm it. It is preposterous on the face of things to proclaim as the inheritors of heaven's graces those who are "as stone." It can be other than ironical only to the cynic, for even the hardhearted man thinks of himself as generous and cherishes an abstract admiration for warmth. In addition, it will be noticed that what Shakespeare says here contradicts everything he has said elsewhere on the subject. The irony of the octave is Swiftian in both method and force. In specious terms the poet states as true that which he is well known to consider false: those men whose appearance does not square with reality, whose deeds do not fulfill their promise, who move others while remaining cold, are proclaimed the heirs to heaven's graces. They are the owners of themselves, whereas throughout Shakespeare's other works self-possession in the sense of living without regard for others is intolerable. After the stinging "Others but stewards of their excellence," there is a full stop, and the poet turns to one of his most familiar images, the flower which is still beautiful although it lives to itself alone. The analogy is obvious. In the opening sequence the flower had been the emblem of the young man "contracted to his own bright eyes." Throughout the sonnets the poet praises the flower for its beauty, which he insists is only one of its attributes, and, he also insists from time to time, not its supreme one. The beauty, he repeats, is made fairer by its odor, which in turn becomes the symbol of that which is usefully good, or of the essential nature of the flower, or of both. In some sonnets the odor, or essence, may be distilled into perfume, in which case its odor will live "pent in walls of glass" after the flower has died. In other instances the distillation of essence is a symbol of procreation. In still others the odor of the flower symbolizes moral good:

> But why thy odor matcheth not thy show,
> The soil this is, that thou dost common grow.

And,

> O, how much more doth beauty beauteous seem
> By that sweet ornament which truth doth give!
> The rose looks fair, but fairer we it deem
> For that sweet odour which in it doth live. . . .

In the sonnet under discussion, the flower living to itself, and having therefore failed to fulfill its function, is incomplete, though it still has physical beauty; but if it should meet with infection (that is, if the expression of its function should be perverted), its odor (that is, its essence, its soul, its human utility expressed in the deeds of the young man and the perfume of the flower) becomes worse than that of weeds, worse, that is, than that from which nothing is expected.

"They that have power to hurt" is both a great poem and an imperfect one. There is neither weakness nor relaxation. It should be noticed that the failure is not, as is often the case, one of fitting the matter to the form. There is neither tacking on nor repetition of matter to fill out a prescribed length. It is rather that the unity is marred by a change in tone, though not in intensity, at the close of the octave, and that the cohesion of parts depends on a context of ideas which are not sufficiently explicit in the poem, though they ought to be familiar to all readers of Shakespeare.

—Edward Hubler, *The Sense of Shakespeare's Sonnets*. (Princeton, NJ: Princeton University Press, 1952), pp. 103–105. ☯

NORTHROP FRYE ON THE YOUTH'S INABILITY TO PRODUCE LOVE

[Northrop Frye, a Canadian educator and literary critic, was the author of *Fearful Symmetry: A Study of William Blake* (1947), an erudite study of Blake's visionary symbolism. In *Anatomy of Criticism*, he stressed the importance of archetypal symbols in literature. His later works include books on T. S. Eliot (1963), Milton's epics (1965), Shakespearean comedy (1965) and tragedy (1967), and English Romanticism (1968). *The Great Code: The Bible and Literature*, a study of the mythology and structure of the Bible, was published in 1982.]

The nadir of experience is represented by the terrible Sonnet 129, which, starting from the thematic words "expense" and "waste," describes what life completely bound to time is like, with the donkey's carrot of passion jerking us along its homeless road, causing an agonizing wrench of remorse at every instant. Directly above is "the heaven that leads men to this hell," and which includes in its many mansions the fool's paradise in which the youth is living in the opening sonnets. Here we must distinguish the poet's tone, which is tender and affectionate, from his imagery, which is disconcertingly sharp. As Sonnet 94 explains in a bitterer context, the youth causes but does not produce love: he is a self-enclosed "bud," contracted to his own bright eyes like Narcissus. As with a child, his self-absorption is part of his charm. He does not need to seek a beauty in women which he already contains (Sonnet 20, where all the rhymes are "feminine"). He lacks nothing, so he is never in search: he merely attracts, even to the point of becoming, in Sonnet 31, a charnel-house of the poet's dead loves. He is therefore not on the side of nature with her interest in "increase," "store," and renewed life, but on the side of time and its devouring "waste." He is his own gradually fading reflection in water, not "A liquid prisoner pent in walls of glass," or a seed which maintains an underground resistance to time. The poet's arguments in Sonnets 1–17 are not intended to be specious, like the similar-sounding arguments of Venus to Adonis. The youth is (by implication at least) "the tomb of his self-love," which is really a hatred turned against himself, and has no future but "folly, age, and cold decay."

—Northrop Frye, "How True a Twain." In *The Riddle of Shakespeare's Sonnets*. (New York: Basic Books, 1962), p. 45.

⊛

STEPHEN BOOTH ON SONNET 94 AND READERS' EXPECTATIONS

[Stephen Booth, Professor of English at the University of California in Berkeley, is the author of *An Essay on Shakespeare's Sonnets*, *The Book Called Holinshed's Chronicles*, and the editor of *Shakespeare's Sonnets*. Booth demonstrates the organization of

Shakespeare's sonnets as a multitude of coexisting but conflicting patterns. The sonnets depend upon a conflict between what is said and what the reader expects.]

All in all, I don't see how any effort to dismiss or subordinate any historically valid reaction evoked by sonnet 94 or any of the other sonnets can be useful or (considering the ability of the sonnets to spring back into shape after undergoing definitive criticism) possible. The essence of this sonnet will not fit into any neat package except the one that it is in. I offer the following loose package as evidence.

They that have pow'r to hurt should not endear themselves to a reader first coming upon them, but *They that have pow'r to hurt and do none* sound like the stuff of heroes. Having the power to hurt makes them sound bad, or at least dangerous; not using it sounds good. This first line describes a dichotomy in the nature of its subjects. The only two qualities it presents for "them" are irrevocably connected and also antipathetic. The line also begins a process of creating a state of mind in the reader in which contrary but inseparable reactions uneasily coexist. The key word in line 1 is *and,* which connects the mutually contradictory impressions in the line as if the second were a straightforward expression of the first. The use of *but* would have presented the reader with a formally structured antithesis that he could have taken in whole. As it is, the reader's attitude toward the subjects of the line is in active flux as he reads it.

In line 1, *that* appears in a perfectly usual relative construction, but in the parallel construction in line 2, *That* is physically so far separated from the grammatical subject as to accentuate the impersonality implied by Shakespeare's use of "that" rather than "who." The word *That* reintroduces the disapprobation dispelled in the previous line by *and will do none.* The reader's coldness toward "them" increases as their own impersonality becomes more evident: *do not do the thing they most do show.* *Thing* is ominously mechanical, and *show* adds a suggestion of theatrical distance and detachment which intensifies the threat inherent in the fact that *the thing they most do show* is the *pow'r to hurt.* On the other hand, the substance of this line is a restatement of another fact: they do no hurt. The double response of the reader is comparable and appropriate to the conflict between the internal and external natures of the subjects of the lines.

At the beginning of the next line *Who,* introducing the third relative clause of the quatrain, simultaneously presents change and continuity; it breaks the pattern established by the preceding *that* clauses, but its vowel sound participates in a phonetic pattern established in the repetitions of *do* in the preceding lines and echoed in *moving.* The hint of comparative humanity in *Who* is also present in *moving others,* which suggests some positive relationship between "them" and other people; in the contexts of the sonnet convention in general, this collection, and the particular poem that precedes this one in the 1609 sequence, *moving others* is likely to suggest that "they" move others by their physical beauty. The reader may be expected at this point to be swaying toward the admiration he felt at the end of line 1, but the completed line brings him back more strongly than ever to the antipathy he felt for "them" at the end of line 2: *Who, moving others, are themselves as stone.*

The next line maintains the reader's antipathy in *Unmovèd, cold.* Between *stone* and *cold, Unmovèd* can only confirm the impression made by those two words, but *to temptation slow* is linked—by another casual *and*—to the series that began with *as stone, Unmovèd,* and *cold.* To be slow to temptation is an admirable quality in any context and one that here suggests another way of evaluating *Unmovèd.* At the same time, however, *to temptation slow* also reflects the idea of enticement back upon *moving others* in line 3. None of the qualities listed in the first quatrain is inconsistent with any other, but the reader's reactions are inconsistent with one another. Unmoved people who are also cold as stone are unfeeling and unadmirable. Unmoved people who are slow to temptation are steadfast and admirable. Shakespeare is not describing the vacillation of a lover, but re-creating a lover's state of mind in the reader by putting him through a miniature but real experience of an attempt to think coherently about people who are both worthy and unworthy objects of admiration.

The syntactical unit begun in line 1 is still incomplete at the end of the first quatrain; the promise of completion is sufficient to push the reader on without pause into quatrain 2. The new quatrain makes a new start on the same statement, repeating the subject and immediately predicating it: *They rightly do inherit heaven's graces.* After evoking such a range of reaction in the subject, the repetition of *They* in line 5 has a forward-thrusting effect comparable to that of the unfinished syntactical unit; in effect, the capability for concrete identification in a pronoun of the people to whom the reader's attitude has been so fluid and unsure gives him a sense of solid grasp on his experience of the poem and gives him the sureness to go on without puzzlement.

It is quite reasonable in this context to expect the reader to hear faint overtones of "as a right" or "as if by right" in *rightly.* Since "they" are so self-controlled, the same is true of the meaning "decorously." Still, the most obvious significance of *rightly do* must be "have a right to," because the usual practice of the language makes a reader expect *rightly* to indicate the speaker's judgment rather than the subejcts' behavior. Moreover, the reader's understanding of *rightly* as indicative of the speaker's approval is heightened by its position in a line that echoes the beatitudes. Still, the assertion that it is right that "they" prosper carries with it the open admission of possible doubt in the matter, and thus confirms the reader's experience of conflicting evidence in quatrain 1. An effect of *rightly* is thus to do what *but* would have done and *and* did not do in lines 1 and 4: it gives rationally graspable form and substance to the contradictions in quatrain 1. The reader gets that comfort, however, after the fact of the experience of the contradictions.

—Stephen Booth, *An Essay on Shakespeare's Sonnets.* (New Haven, CT: Yale University Press, 1969), pp. 159–163.

HAROLD BLOOM ON SONNET 94 AS A FORERUNNER TO SHAKESPEARE'S TRAGEDIES

[Harold Bloom is Sterling Professor of the Humanities at Yale University and Berg Professor of English at New York University. He is the author of more than 20 books, including the best-selling *The Western Canon* (1994) and *The Book of J* (1990), and is the editor of over 400 anthologies of both literature and literary criticism. His works include *Shelley's Mythmaking* (1959), *Blake's Apocalypse* (1963), *Yeats* (1970), *A Map of Misreading* (1975), *Kabbalah and Criticism* (1975), *Wallace Stevens: The Poems of Our Climate* (1977), *Agon: Towards a Theory of Revisionism* (1982), *American Religion* (1992), and *Omens of Millennium*(1996). *The Anxiety of Influence* (1973) sets forth Bloom's theory of the literary relationships between great writers and their predecessors.]

Is there an equivalent in Shakespeare's Sonnets to his most original power as a dramatist: to represent changes in his characters as ensuing from what they overhear themselves say, whether to others or to themselves? Does the condensed art of a sonnet allow Shakespeare to become one of his own characters, as it were, caught in the process of changing as a reaction to, or reflection of, his own utterance? I do not mean to ask again how dramatic the sonnets are or are not. Rather, I wonder if any among the Sonnets fulfull A. D. Nuttall's fine assertion for Shakespearean mimesis, that it makes us see aspects of reality we never could have seen without it.

The aesthetic strength of the Sonnets has little to do with their appearance in a sequence, as more seems to be lost than gained when we read them straight through in order. As a rough series of isolated splendors, the best among them are rightly judged to be the most eminent in the language, superior not only to Spenser, Sidney, and Drayton, but also to Milton, Wordsworth, and Keats. They have a monumental quality difficult to match in any Western language, worthy of the poet of "The Phoenix and the Turtle."

Not many critics have preferred Sonnet 94 to all the other sonnets, but it has intrigued nearly every commentator because of its ambivalences:

> They that have the pow'r to hurt, and will do none,
> They that do not do the thing they most do show,
> Who moving others, are themselves as stone,
> Unmoved, cold, and to temptation slow,
> They rightly do inherit heaven's graces,
> And husband nature's riches from expense;
> They are the lords and owners of their faces,
> Others but stewards of their excellence.
> The summer's flow'r is to the summer sweet,
> Though to itself it only live and die,
> But if that flow'r with base infection meet,
> The basest weed outbraves his dignity:
>> For sweetest things turn sourest by their deeds;
>> Lilies that fester smell far worse than weeds.

Stephen Booth sees this as a "stylistic mirror of the speaker's indecision," and observes that "The sentences wander from attribute to attribute in such a way that the reader's response to 'them' who are the subject of lines 1–8 swings repeatedly back and forth between negative and positive." The crucial question then would be: Is the speaker's indecision resolved through the implications of the couplet ending the poem? But that in turn depends upon another question: how undecided truly is the speaker in regard to "them"?

If you choose not to hurt someone else, even as your outward semblance intimates you are almost certainly about to do so, there may be a considerable touch of sadomasochism in you. Or you may be like Hamlet, who most provokes the love of the audience in act 5, where he is beyond the reach of love. An unmoved mover is more a divinity than a magnet, and so rightly inherits heaven's graces. So far at least the poem that I encounter is no mirror of its speaker's supposed indecision.

To "husband nature's riches from expense" *may* mean to hold one's sexuality in reserve, to abstain from expending it, but I am reluctant, in the context of Sonnet 94, to so restrict the sense of "nature's riches." We think of Hamlet as one of nature's great treasures because we think of him as an adventure of and in the spirit. In act 5, he manifests extraordinary disinterestedness; are we so far from that Hamlet if we speak of him as husbanding nature's riches from expense? In full and final control, the Hamlet of act 5 indeed is the lord and owner of his face, the outward image that he turns to Elsinore and to the audience. That brings us to the puzzling line: "Others but stewards of their excellence," where the emphasis upon "their" clearly gives us not "others" but "lords and owners" as the antecedent. To continue with my Hamlet analogue, Horatio is a prime instance of one of those stewards of excellence, who survive to tell the story of the greater figures they admire and love.

On this reading, then, the hero, Hamlet or another, is "the summer's flow'r," sweet to Horatio and the audience, but essentially living and dying by and for himself, for ends we can only partly apprehend, let alone accept. The crisis of meaning turns upon the nature of the base infection that the hero meets. I do not accept a reading that associates the infection with the weed, for the "base" in "base infection" means "debasing" or potentially debasing, whereas "the basest weed" is already debased. Think of poor Othello as summer's flower debased by the infection of jealous madness, and so fallen into the terrible lack of dignity of his madness at its incoherent worst. Hamlet is precisely a being who is not turned sourest by his deeds, not a lily that festers.

I hardly seek to turn the Sonnets (1592 to 1596, or so) into a prophecy of *Hamlet* (1600 to 1601) or rather say of *Othello* (1604), but Sonnet 94 is emblematic of the tragedian who was to come, unless indeed it was written later than most of the other sonnets, which is possible enough. On my reading, it is the negative equivalent of what Wordsworth celebrated when he chanted that feeling comes in aid of feeling, and diversity of strength attends us if but once we have been strong. Strength, in Shakespeare, becomes horror when feeling comes to prey upon feeling, and Othello and Macbeth fall into ruin the more dreadfully because, in their different ways, they were so strong.

I do not find then the ambivalences in Sonnet 94 that so many, including Empson, have found, and so I do not find the speaker changing in the final couplet. I would suppose then that the Sonnets, even at their strongest, are indeed lyric rather than dramatic, marvelously conventional rather than personally expressive. Wordsworth and Keats learn from Shakespeare in their sonnets, but are closer to Milton because they put into their sonnets, as Milton sometimes did, the burden of their prophecy. Shakespeare, who had the power to hurt, nevertheless husbanded nature's riches from expense in his Sonnets and chose rather to live and die not only to himself, in his tragedies.

—Harold Bloom, Introduction to *Shakespeare's Sonnets*, ed. Harold Bloom. (New York: Chelsea House Publishers, 1987), pp. 1–3.

HELEN VENDLER ON SHAKESPEARE'S USE OF PLANT METAPHORS IN SONNET 94

[Helen Vendler is the A. Kingsley Porter University Professor at Harvard University. Her previous books include *Yeats' Vision and the Later Plays* (1963) and *On Extended Wings: Wallace Stevens' Longer Poems* (1969). Her most recent book is *The Art of Shakespeare's Sonnets* (1997), from which this extract is taken.]

This powerful and much-commented-upon poem, turning oddly from *pow'r* to *flow'r* (lines 1, 9), is remarkable for its structural experiment, by which Shakespeare "splits" the couplet into two separate lines, each of which gives closure to a different segment of the poem. Line 13 sums up the human octave of *pow'r*, which turns on the word do and its derivative deeds; line 14 sums up the vegetative quatrain of *flow'r*, which turns on a botanical hierarchy of *weeds* and their vegetative superiors (in general, flowers, specifically lilies). The sonnet thus contains two mini-poems, represented by the several elements of the Couplet Tie: *do* [*deeds*] and *thing*[*-s*] for the first, human mini-poem; *weed*[*-s*] for the second, vegetative one; and *sweet*[*-est*] as the ambiguous Couplet Tie belonging to both mini-poems, linking people and flowers. . . .

The speaker's powerful set of mixed responses to the beautiful but indifferent young man has led to a self-protective retreat from the social to the vegetative realm—to the invention of the flower and its adoring summer. But contaminating that idyllic scene—drawn from the lilies of the field of Jesus' parable—is the repressed suspicion of 93, that the infection of the flower has already taken place. By phrasing this intuition as a hypothesis ("But *if* that flow'r"), the speaker attempts to preserve his sweet flower, and to blame, in the event his suspicions prove true, the flower's corruption on a meeting with *base infection*, the villain of the piece. The speaker admits that he himself is a *base weed* by comparison to his aloof *flow'r*; but even if he should be the *basest* weed, he would be higher in the order of vegetation than an infected flower. There is a retort to the young man here embedded in the word *outbraves*: "You have in the past scorned me (perhaps defensibly); but if you have now sinned, your sweetness is lost, and I outrank you in dignity." The double superlatives predicated of *things* (*sweetest, sourest*) act out the proverbial corruption of the best into the worst, and connect semantically and phonetically the *sour* (formerly *sweet*) *flow'r* to the *pow'r* of the octave. The concluding proverb revealingly leaves out any mention at all of *base infection:* lilies can fester (in the sense of "decay") all by themselves. The retaliatory overturning of normal vegetative hierarchy in the last line is connected to *outbraves* in Q₃, while the lingering look at deeds in the penultimate line connects its *sweetest things*—a last nostalgia—to the undone "shown" *thing* which now—unspecified—must have been *done.* (Cf. *Othello,* to "do the deed of darkness.")

The shift from *pow'r* to the alternate venue of flower-metaphor has been proved unavailing: both "lines of thought," the social one and the flower one, have ended up in the same place, a place where no excuses for the young man persist. By *deeds, things* have become *sour,* and festering flowers *smell worse* than the weeds around them. With the failure of 94's hopeful diversion into organic metaphor, the accusations suppressed in 93 and 94 can burst out in full cry in 95: *O what a mansion have those vices got / Which for their habitation chose out thee!* The fiction of the external villain that *chose out* and corrupted the young man is hard to maintain, but still clings in 95. The sternness of tone in 94—a tone not of infatuation but of social reproof and moral authority—grows in the sequence from its origin in such poems as 66 through its exertions in 94 on to such famous sonnets as 116, 124, and 129.

—Helen Vendler, *The Art of Shakespeare's Sonnets.* (Cambridge, MA: Harvard University Press, 1997), pp. 403–406.

Sonnet 116

MURRAY KRIEGER ON POETRY AS A TESTAMENT TO IMMORTALITY

[Murray Krieger was Professor of English at the University of California in Los Angeles until 1982. He is the author of *The Tragic Vision: Variations on a Theme in Literary Interpretation* (1960), *The Play and Place of Criticism* (1967), *The Classic Vision: The Retreat from Extremity in Modern Literature* (1971), and *Poetic Presence and Illusion: Essays in Critical History and Theory.* He is also the author of *A Window to Criticism: Shakespeare's Sonnets and Modern Poetics,* from which this extract is taken. Krieger suggests that Shakespeare's Sonnets comprise a "memorial tomb of love to which, as a womb, it gives eternal life" (193). He finds in the Sonnets a key to the nature of poetry and poetics, and focuses on their mirror-window metaphorical system.]

Love as "the marriage of true minds" reminds us that we are in the world of troth. Thus there must be no "impediments" to this marriage since only a subject of time can be forced to cooperate with time to produce an impediment. The cooperation with time is verbally enforced by the effective repetition that has time's fool following upon the aging action ("alters when it alteration finds") and the destructive action ("bends with the remover to remove") of time and his sickle. The seconding action this repetition suggests is especially persuasive in contrast to the use of repetition, joined by "not" in order to negate—even expunge—in the preceding line ("Love is not love"). There is the further repetition of forms of "bend" and "alter" in lines 10 and 11, giving a reverse or mirror-image of lines 3 and 4, (and, among other things, reinforcing the sickle image of line 4). The third quatrain, as an intensified echo of the first, presses the negative definition of love, of which we have not seen a more sustained instance in Sonnet 124. Love will not add its destruction to that of the "rosy lips and cheeks," but rather asserts its eternal fixity. Here in the third quatrain, as in the echoes of lines 3 and 4, we are once more in the world of Sonnet 71 (and the line, "But let your love even with my life decay"). This reminds us of the opposition between truth and troth, time's truth and love's. . . . So it is not surprising that, when Shakespeare does introduce a positive definition in the second quatrain, he insists on a value for the star beyond the futile measurability of fact: "Whose worth's unknown, although his highth be taken." His extravagance—anti-scientific, may we call it?—is of course beyond logic as well as fact. Yet, as if in defiance of logic and fact, the unreasonable reason of love asserts its own version of logic and fact in the pseudo-syllogism of the couplet. The fact is the existence of this very sonnet, which is to prove that the poet has indeed "writ." The tactic here may remind us of the argumentative factuality of the "this" in Sonnet 74, lines 5–6 ("When thou reviewest this, thou dost review / The very part was consecrate to thee") and the couplet ("The worth of that is that which it contains, / And that this is, and this with thee remains"), which I have discussed earlier in these terms. The logic there is similar too: the fact of this poem is guarantor of the poet's faith ("the very part was consecrate to thee"), of the immaterial "spirit," and of his true (that is, trothful) "worth."

Here, in Sonnet 116, the fact of his having written is the proof of his having loved. Love's faith is constituted by the poem, the one mirror-window testifying to the other. The testament of love is the embassy of poetry. As an aesthetically successful mirror-window, the sovereign entity which is the poem is "hugely politic," the body politic of Sonnet 124, which becomes the material proof as it is the domain, the physical realm, of love. Yet, together with love, it is exempt from man's "state" so that it too is no fool of time. Thus in Sonnet 116, as in Sonnet 74 and elsewhere, Shakespeare does more than borrow the Petrarchan convention of defying mortality through verse: by using the fact of this poem he matches the materialism of mortality and its truth with the materialism of immortality and its troth, with verse—the spirit made word and thing—the incarnation and thus the living proof of the immaterial world. The confident, absolute tone of the couplet is further ensured by the unqualified opposites of eternity, "never" and "ever," especially as these repeat the earlier opposition between them in lines 5 and 6. But nothing less absolute can do for the pure logic of love's reason, with its total identity of faith and the word, of faith in the word.

—Murray Krieger, *A Window to Criticism.* (Princeton, NJ: Princeton University Press, 1964), pp. 146–150.

☙

RICHARD LANHAM ON RHETORIC AND THE TRUTH OF LOVE IN SONNET 116

[Richard Lanham, Professor of English at the University of California in Los Angeles, is the author of *Sidney's Old Arcadia, Handlist of Rhetorical Terms, Tristram Shandy: The Games of Pleasure,* and *Revising Prose and Analyzing Prose.* He is also the author of *Motives of Eloquence: Literary Rhetoric in the Renaissance* (1976), from which this extract is taken.]

Is the final couplet paradoxical? Doesn't it rather make two different kinds of statements in the same words? If "nor no man ever loved" is a private statement, topical reference, private audience, it means one thing. If a public statement—not "I never loved any man" but "No man ever loved anybody"—then it says something else. The couplet illustrates perfectly the sonnets' characteristic reasoning. The "proof" runs this way. "If such ever-constant love is a delusion, then I have never writ. But since I have manifestly writ, then it must be true." Reality, the chain of reasoning, the only undeniable premise, however absurd, is the act of writing. Style, the act of writing, again forms both center and surface. Not writing the truth, since he admits in line one of 115, "Those lines that I before have writ do lie," but the act of writing. On this premise is built true love. Or, if writing again is the only *undeniable* reality, if true love really is a delusion—and the previous one hundred fifteen sonnets have shown Shakespeare's love shaken, removed, unfixed, full of nothing but impediments—then, following the "logic," some other "I" must have written them. No problem. One hundred fifteen other "I's," at least, stand ready. Neither central self nor true love finally supplies the referent reality. Shakespeare in sonnet 116 argues a case for rhetorical coordinates, as well as against them. *Amo ergo sum* on the one hand; *Scribo ergo sum* on the other. Read as a serious poem, it argues that the "star," love, is a necessary assumption if the world is to make any sense. We must start with some commitment. Why not call it Love. *Amo ergo sum.* Read within rhetorical coordinates, it says that all you really start with is the act of writing. *Scribo ergo sum.* The poem is about the relation between the two poetics. A poem about defining essence—the marriage of true minds—it yet leans on its words in such a way, varying their sense with repetition, that essence dwells first in words: Love, love; alters, alteration; remover, remove. Is such a subject serious? It is and it isn't. The poem seems at once the most profound and the most playful in the sequence. Two different poems share the same words.

> —Richard Lanham, *The Motives of Eloquence: Literary Rhetoric in the Renaissance.* (New Haven, CT: Yale University Press, 1976), pp. 124–125.

✍

STEPHEN BOOTH ON SUBSTANCE AND EMPTINESS IN SONNET 116

[Stephen Booth, Professor of English at the University of California in Berkeley, is the author of *An Essay on Shakespeare's Sonnets, The Book Called Holinshed's Chronicles,* and the editor of *Shakespeare's Sonnets,* from which this extract is taken. Booth demonstrates the organization of Shakespeare's sonnets as a multitude of coexisting but conflicting patterns. The sonnets depend upon a conflict between what is said and what the reader expects.]

Sonnet 116 is the most universally admired of Shakespeare's sonnets. Its virtues, however, are more than usually susceptible to dehydration in critical comment. The more one thinks about this grand, noble, absolute, convincing, and moving gesture, the less there seems to be to it. One could demonstrate that it is just so much bombast, but, having done so, one would have only to reread the poem to be again moved by it and convinced of its greatness.

A major problem about literary art is that abstract general assertions do no feel any truer than their readers already believe them to be; they carry no evidence of their truth and very little of the life (and thus very little of the undeniability) of the physically extant particulars from which they derive. Descriptions of those particulars, or exempla, or metaphoric allusions can bring life and conviction to a generalization, but they also limit its range and its value to the reader. The attraction of abstract generalizations is the capacity they offer us to be *certain o'er incertainty* (115.11), to fix on a truth that allows for and cannot be modified by further consideration of experience or change in our angle of vision. One means of achieving universality and vividness at once is bombast: high sounding, energetic nonsense that addresses its topic but does not indicate what is being said about it, and thus rises free of human intellectual limitations like a hot-air balloon. Bombast, however, is rarely satisfying for long or to any listener who pays attention to the signification of the words he hears strung together. Bombast overcomes the difficulties of language by abandoning its purpose; a general, noble, vibrant utterance that conveys no meaning operates like a bureaucracy that functions perfectly so long as it ignores the purpose for which it was established.

Sonnet 116 has simple clear content; indeed, its first clause aside, it is one of the few Shakespeare sonnets that can be paraphrased without brutality.

That alone excludes it from classification as bombast, but much of its strength and value is of the same sort that bombast has. Sonnet 116 achieves effective definition unlimited by any sense of effective limitation. One obvious source of that success is its positiveness is achieved in negative assertions (a definition by negatives is minimally restrictive because the thing so defined may be thought to possess all qualities but those specifically denied). Some of the means by which negative definition is made efficient, convincing, and satisfying in this sonnet are those that can be used to give grandeur to nonsense.

The sonnet combines extreme generality—even vagueness—with locutions that imply some degree of personification and thus invest abstract statements with the urgency, vividness, and apprehensibility of concrete particulars. . . .

None of that is at all complicated until it is explained. The lines do not demand any explanation; they are immediately clear, but they derive much of their power from being both simple and straightforward and simultaneously so complexly wondrous that beholder and beheld are indistinguishable from one another in a statement that makes their ordinary relationship perfectly clear.

A similar blend of substantial and insubstantial fabric occurs on a larger scale in *Love is not love* (line 2) and in *I never writ, nor no man ever loved* (line 14). In these two cases the speaker's meaning is clear and immediate, uncolored by the incidental supernaturalness inherent in metaphoric perception; at the same time, both assert absolute nonsense. *Love is not love* is a traditional (and traditionally pleasing) kind of incidental paradox in which a straightforward assertion (in this case, "That kind of love is not genuine love") is phrased so as to be meaningless if taken literally. Similarly, the hyperbole of the couplet is so extreme that it merely vouches for the speaker's intensity of feeling; it gives no evidence to support the validity of his statement because on a literal level it is ridiculous (we cannot doubt that what we read was written). Moreover, though the special meaning "truly loved" is obvious in *no man ever loved*, that assertion, like *Love is not love*, gets its rhetorical power from the ostentatious falsehood of its unmodified literal sense.

The discussion of Shakespeare's devices for simultaneously emhpasizing particularity and vagueness, substance and emptiness, brings us to a related technique in sonnet 116 that has related effects: the poem is both single-minded, presenting constancy as the only matter worth considering, and heterogeneous in ways that do nothing to diminish or intrude upon its sin-glemindedness. In examining the special appeal of sonnet 116, it may be well to remember that in saying anything—no matter how general—one advertises the fact that one has not said everything else—everything else pertinent to one's topic and everything else impertinent to one's topic. That may sound less simpleminded and more worth saying if one considers the related proposition that the literary creations we value most are works like *Hamlet, King Lear, Paradise Lost,* and *Ulysses,* works so full—so full of matter, so full of different kinds of matter, and so open to being viewed from so many angles of vision—that their particulars seem to include all particulars, and the experience of them seems to take in all experience and all attitudes toward it. Sonnet 116 is overlaid with relationships established in patterning factors that do not pertain to or impinge upon the logic and syntax of the particular authoritative statement it makes. The most obvious of them, of course, are the formal iambic pentameter rhythmic pattern and the sonnet rhyme scheme. This sonnet, however, also contains patterns of a kind that falls between the ideational structure (what the poem says) and the substantively irrelevant phonetic patterns of the sonnet form: patterns established by the relationship of the meanings of its words—in this case meanings that are irrelevant to, and do not color, the particular sentences in which they appear here but which do pertain generally to the topic about which the sentences isolate particular truths in particular frames of reference.

—Stephen Booth, ed., *Shakespeare's Sonnets.* (New Haven, CT: Yale University Press, 1977), pp. 389–390.

☙

LOWRY NELSON JR. ON THE STRENGTH OF SHAKESPEARE'S RHYME IN SONNET 116

[Lowry Nelson Jr., late Professor of Comparative Literature at Yale University, is the author of *Baroque Lyric Poetry* (1961) and "The Fictive Reader and Literary Self-reflexiveness."]

As a conscientious poet Shakespeare had the conviction of his rimes, and in some clear cases was put to shifts to make the sense and rhythm come out at least acceptably. A common fault in rimed poetry—which Shakespeare in his best sonnets worked to avoid—is, as I have noted, the lame relative clause or descriptive phrase that could better have been a single word. It is, of course, difficult to distinguish padding from convincing colloquial prolixity; besides, extreme compression can well be a fault, as it is in quite a few of Shakespeare's sonnets that have to many seemed obscure. In this regard it is interesting to compare Sonnets 55 and 116, the first in the *exegi monumentum* vein, the second on the constancy of love. In 55 we read, as the poem exaltedly and rather verbosely flows,

> . . . your praise shall still find room
> Even in the eyes of all posterity
> That wear this world out to the ending doom.

The rime and the notion are accommodated. Yet the last line given here seems rhythmically weak and too long as an enjambed descriptive clause, lamely and otiosely modifying "doom" with "ending." In 116, which perhaps begins less strikingly, we find "doom" (which I take to be a true rime here in Shakespeare's pronunciation) again in the same position at the end of the twelfth line:

> Love's not Time's fool, though rosy lips and cheeks
> Within his bending sickle's compass come;
> Love alters not with his brief hours and weeks,
> But bears it out even to the edge of doom.

Here, to begin with, the clause is independent and the verb-phrase "bears it out" is not weakened by a long object ("it" vs. "this world"). The trochaic stress on "even" tilts the line toward a strong conclusion with two climactic stresses on "edge" and "doom." Thus the word "doom," resonant in both sound and sense, can express its full and elemental import. Incidentally the rhythmic force, to my ear, shortens "even" to "evn." These two passages are clearly related, not so much in subject matter or sense as in sound and technique. We are in Shakespeare's ear.

—Lowry Nelson, Jr., "The Matter of Rime." In *Poetic Traditions of the English Renaissance*, ed. Maynard Mack and George deForest Lord. (New Haven and London: Yale University Press, 1982), pp. 135–136.

☙

JOSEPH PEQUIGNEY ON THE POET'S LOVE FOR THE YOUTH VERSUS HIS LUST FOR THE MISTRESS

[Joseph Pequigney is Professor of English at the State University of New York at Stony Brook. In his book *Such Is My Love: A Study of Shakespeare's Sonnets*, from which this extract is taken, Pequigney argues that the sonnet sequence represents "the grand masterpiece of homoerotic poetry." He describes a complex and psychologically realistic story of the poet's erotic attachment to the fair young man of Sonnets 1–126. Sonnets 127–154, dealing with the dark lady, are read as a footnote to the jealousy crisis described in sonnets 40–42. The first 126 sonnets depict a sexual relationship between the poet and the youth that complies with Freud's views on homosexuality.]

The way of being in love described in Sonnet 116 and realized through most of Part 1 is one that entails an interaction of "affectionate" emotions with the sexual instinct, or, as Freud puts it, as "synthesis between the unsensual, heavenly love and the sensual, earthly love," of which the characteristics are these: "a lasting cathexis upon the sexual object," so that it may be loved "in the passionless intervals" between the gratification of erotic desire and its return, "the phenomenon of sexual overvaluation," and a narcissistic relation to the subject's ego. Sexual overvaluation, or the "tendency" toward "idealization," means that "the loved object enjoys a certain amount of freedom from criticism," that "its characteristics are valued more highly than those of people not loved," and that, "if the sensual impulses are more or less repressed or set aside, the illusion is produced that the object has come to be loved on account of its spiritual merits," whereas the converse may be true, that these merits have been "lent to it by its sensual charm." Moreover, the lover treats the loved object just as he does himself, so that "a considerable amount of narcissistic libido overflows" onto it, and "in many forms of love-choice," among which the sonneteer's homosexual form would certainly be included, "the object serves as a substitute for some unattained ego ideal," being loved "on account of perfections" the subject has wanted and can now acquire by being in love, a "roundabout" means of "satisfying his narcissism."

All of these characteristics, it hardly needs saying at this point, belong to the poet's love for the friend. It is a love that pays handsome narcissistic dividends, is steady, and is, as the "star" at 116.7, heavenly; it is advantageous also for the friend, who is praised and prized for personal qualities that would likely pass unnoticed were the poet not under the spell of his beauty. The mistress, on the other hand, offers no narcissistic advantages; she is disesteemed, with vice but never virtue ascribed to her; even her physical attractiveness is more and more impugned as the affair proceeds; and she arouses lust that comes and goes.

When Sonnets 116 and 129 are read in place in Q, additional contrasts between them appear. The friend is not addressed in 116 but is addressed in the adjacent sonnets, and the same is true of the mistress in 129, who is not addressed there but is addressed immediately before and after. Sonnet 116 is undoubtedly intended for the eyes of the friend, for why should so eloquent a disquisition on the "marriage" in which he participates be kept from him? Besides, Sonnet 115, which does speak directly to him, likewise expresses the continuousness of love. Sonnet 129 can hardly be intended for the eyes of the mistress, for she could only be appalled by its contents. Besides, the theme is sharply at odds with that of Sonnet 128, which woos her, and of 130, which pays her a compliment—one she would hardly be receptive to after seeing 129. Text and context indicate that in Sonnet 116 the poet is mindful of the other "true mind" espoused to his and that in Sonnet 129 the personality of the lady, his accessory in lust, is remote from his consciousness.

—Joseph Pequigney, *Such Is My Love: A Study of Shakespeare's Sonnets*. (Chicago: University of Chicago Press, 1985), pp. 180–183.

HELEN VENDLER ON SONNET 116 AS A REBUTTAL

[Helen Vendler is the A. Kingsley Porter University Professor at Harvard University. Her previous books include *Yeats' Vision and the Later Plays* (1963) and *On Extended Wings: Wallace Stevens' Longer Poems* (1969). Her most recent book is *The Art of Shakespeare's Sonnets* (1997), from which this extract is taken.]

This famous almost "impersonal" sonnet on the marriage of true minds has usually been read as a definition of true love. That is, most readers decide to see the poem (guided by its beginning) as an example of the genre of definition, and this initial genre-decision generates their interpretation. Let me begin by saying that I read this poem as an example not of definition but of dramatic refutation or rebuttal.

The aesthetic motivation governing 116 springs (as I hope to show) from the fiction of an anterior utterance by another which the sonnet is concerned to repudiate. My interpretation—suggesting that the usual interpretation is untrue, and not simply incomplete—springs from reading along a line of difference: the quatrains differ powerfully from one another. Also, there are too many *no's* and *nor's*, *never's* and *not's* in this poem—one *nor*, two *no's*, two *never's*, and four *not's*—for it to seem a serene one. The prevalence of negation suggests that this poem is not a definition, but rather a rebuttal—and all rebuttals encapsulate the argument they refute. As we can deduce the prior utterance being rebutted (one made, it seems reasonable to assert, by the young man), it has gone roughly as follows:

> "You would like the marriage of minds to have the same permanence as the sacramental marriage of bodies. But this is unreasonable—there are impediments to such constancy. After all, persons alter; and when one finds alteration, one is himself bound to alter as well; and also, people (or some qualities in them) leave, and others remove. I did love you once, but you have altered, and so there is a natural alteration in me."

It is the iambic prosody that first brings the pressure of rhetorical refutation into Shakespeare's line: "Let *me* not to the marriage of true minds / Admit impediments." The speaker says these lines schematically, mimicking, as in reported discourse, his interlocutor's original iron laws of expediency in human intercourse: "To find alteration is to alter; to see a removal is to remove." (This law is, on the part of the young man, a self-exculpating move; we see it in a grim parody of the laws of true reciprocity proposed throughout the *Sonnets*.) And yet we are struck by the dreadful plausibility of the young man's laws: they read like laws of mathematics. Alter the left side of the equation, and you will alter the right; remove X from the left, and of course something must vanish from the right. Alteration causes altering; removers cause removing.

On the other hand, it is not very clear what the young man had in mind in framing his laws. What is all this vague talk of altering and removing? Of course one who argues as the young man does has something specific in mind (usually a new erotic attachment), but prefers to cloud it under large self-excusing generalizations. And the one who disingenuously argues for "impediments" must have some of his own in mental reserve. . . .

Without the differential model of refutation, reinscription, and authorial rethinking, the poem is perfectly seen; we cannot judge its representational aim. No reader, to my knowledge, has seen *Let me not to the marriage of true minds* as a coherent refutation of the extended implied argument of an opponent, and this represents an astonishing history of critical oversight, a paradigmatic case of how reading a poem as though it were an essay, governed by an initial topic sentence, can miss its entire aesthetic dynamic. Because many readers still seek, in the anxiety of reading, a reassuring similarity of patterning among quatrains rather than a perplexing difference, and prefer to think of the *Sonnets* as discursive propositional statements rather than as situationally motivated speech-acts, we remain condemned to a static view of any given sonnet. It is as useful to ask of each sonnet what form of speech-act it performs as to ask what aesthetic problems generated the poem as their exfoliated display; but these are not the same question, though they are often related. Here, the speech-act we call refutation could equally well, for instance, have been carried out entirely in the first person, as it is in the following sonnet

(*Accuse me thus*). To discuss the aesthetic problems set by Shakespeare writing the sonnet, we must first ask the reason in decorum for the use of the impersonal definition-form governing the middle ten lines; next the reason for the necessity of doubling the definition-form, so as to offer negative definitions as well as positive ones; and third, why the negative-positive arrangement had to be done *twice*, so as to make two negative and two positive refutations in lieu of one of each. There are various answers to these problems; I am concerned only that they should be named as problems. We can perhaps see the indecorum of insisting entirely in the first-person singular on the exclusive worth of one's own fashion of loving (though the speaker resorts to that move in the couplet); but the problem of the two refutations doubled is a more interesting one, as is the necessity for the reinscription (as I have called it) of the young man's vague words (*alter, bend*) in the full clarity of their exposure as they are given, in the person of the grim reaper, emblematic form.

The chilling impersonality of the hideous implied "law of alteration and removal" gives a clue to the sort of language used by the young man which is here being refuted, just as the speaker's first refutational metaphor, the metaphor of transcendent worth, establishes another form of diction wholly opposed to the young man's sordid algebraic diction of proportional alteration. The second refutational passage, in the third quatrain, proposes indirectly a valuable alternative law, one approved by the poet-speaker, which we may label "the law of inverse constancy": the more inconstant are time's alterations (one an hour, one a week), the more constant is love's endurance, even to the edge of doom. The impersonal phraseology of law, at first the young man's euphemistic screen for his own infidelity, is triumphantly but tragically modified by the speaker into the law of constancy in trial. That is, the reinscription (using *alters* and *bending*, adapted from *alters, alteration*, and *bends*), not only brings out the latent significance of these euphemistically disguising words, but also (by proposing a different "universal" law) reinscribes with new significance the very structural form (an invariant law) of the young man's objections. The model which I call "reinscription," then, consists here of a first message about alteration and bending inscribed in the implied form of a self-serving law, and a second message about alteration and bending inscribed in the form of a constancy-law. We can now see why the transcendent metaphorical star alone could not refute the young man: he had to be refuted in his own temporal and metonymic terms, as the identical form (a "law" of physical necessity) of the reinscribed message indicates.

The young man, by his mentioning of "impediments," has announced the waning of his own attachment to the speaker, dissolving the "marriage of true minds." It is not surprising to see, in the following sonnets, the young man's attempts to project the blame for his own faithlessness on the speaker (117), and the speaker, taking his cue, acting out his own infidelities (118).

—Helen Vendler, *The Art of Shakespeare's Sonnets*. (Cambridge, MA: Harvard University Press, 1997), pp. 488–489. ☙

Sonnet 129

RICHARD LEVIN ON THE EVOLUTION OF EMOTION IN SONNET 129

[Richard Levin, Professor of English Literature at State University of New York at Stony Brook, is the author of *The Multiple Plot in English Renaissance Drama* and "New Reading vs. Old Plays in Recent Trends" in *Reinterpretation of English Renaissance Drama*.]

There is, however, a different critical approach that would not accept such assumptions, but would hold that the sonnet can be analyzed more fruitfully in *dramatic* terms, much as one would analyze a soliloquy in a play. If we are prepared to examine it from this perspective—to see it, that is, not as Shakespeare's "disquisition" upon an abstract topic, but as his attempt to render the response, at once emotional and intellectual, of a certain kind of man in a concrete situation—then I believe it will be found to have an extremely effective structure, one which corresponds to the metrical divisions and also to our own experience of the poem. Regarded in this light, the sonnet presents an easily understood dramatic situation: in it a man (the "speaker" of these lines) is reacting with bitter disgust to a recent sexual encounter. It is also easy, from this viewpoint, to understand and appreciate the overall movement of the poem, since we will not be looking for a logical, nontemporal progression of parts (as in a syllogism, for example), but for a psychological development through time. Therefore, the obvious diminution of energy in the second and third quatrains and the relative lameness of the conclusion can now be explained, not as failures in Shakespeare's constructive powers or poetic inspiration, but as his very vivid representation of the inevitable dissipation of the speaker's revulsion once the initial impetus plays itself out. Even the stages of this movement now become comprehensible, for the emotion does not discharge in an orderly sequence of descending steps, but through abrupt fits and starts gradually decreasing in impact, as would be expected of a person undergoing this particular kind of experience.

This mode of analysis, then, will explain why the poem begins at its moment of greatest intensity, in what is certainly the most violent opening in all of Shakespeare's sonnets. The first clause is a sudden outburst of disgust, an unqualified condemnation of the entire act of lust that the speaker now looks back upon, which is made especially emphatic by the piling up of explosive, almost spitting consonantal combinations, and by the reversal of normal syntax, starting with the predicate that carries the actual impact of the speaker's emotion (as if it were too overpowering to await its place in a "logically" thought out proposition), and delaying the subject just long enough to hold the reader in suspense and draw him immediately into the action which seems to unfold in *medias res*. Then, turning rapidly upon "and" as a fulcrum, the remainder of the quatrain attacks the anticipatory stage of lust, the stage that seems most repulsive to this man, now physically sated, when he remembers all that has been done for the sake of his empty fulfillment. Here his self-laceration finds expression in a series of adjectives that come tumbling out (in marked contrast to the unbroken sweep of the first clause) in a jerky, staccato rhythm, like a barrage of verbal blows, suggesting at once the extremity of his rage and also, indirectly, its impotence, since it can only strike out at its object in this way. The order within these two lines helps to establish this undertone of futility, for in each line the final epithet is milder than those preceding it (and is further weakened since it is broken into three monosyllables, two of which are affectively neutral), and the fourth line finishes more mildly than the third. This slight attenuation at the end of the quatrain prepares for and initiates the movement already noted in the sonnet as a whole.

The second quatrain carries this movement further. It begins with the first qualification of the speaker's revulsion, his admission in line five, quickly passed over, that lust is "Enjoy'd". This refers to the moment of consummation, and line six glances at the anticipatory stage developed earlier, but the quatrain concentrates primarily on the aftermath of lust, the stage he is experiencing now. Having expressed his guilty reaction to past activity, he is here reacting to that reaction, and this turning in upon himself removes him another step from the immediacy and the violence of his initial outburst. The explosive sound effects are gone, the tempo has smoothed out considerably, and balanced antitheses are more prominent. One such construction had been set up in line two of the first quatrain, but the parallelism there was abruptly broken—as if the emotional pressures were too great to complete it—by the surge of adjectives that followed. The second quatrain, however, opens with two carefully balanced oppositions ("Enjoy'd ... despised"; "Past reason hunted . . . Past reason hated"), and although the second is then thrown off by a run-on clause, the shift in syntax and rhythm is much less drastic than in the first quatrain, indicating that the inner turmoil has decreased.

In the third quatrain, these parallel constructions become the dominant feature. Each of the four lines is built in this way, with its parts nicely balanced syntactically and metrically, and the oppositions or equations underscored by alliteration, assonance, traduction, and other standard tropes. Such perfect control of the medium of expression implies control over the affective content; because of it we sense a definite weakening of the emotional stresses within the speaker, and a corresponding increase in his intellectual mastery of his experience. The fact that in this quatrain, for the first time, all the lines are end-stopped tends to enhance this impression (as does the unusual initial rhyme of "Mad" and "Had", which also seems to emphasize the discreteness of these two lines), not only by sharply framing each of the four balanced clauses within its own self-contained line, but, again, by showing that the emotions no longer press so insistently to break through the verse unit. It is also significant (and another consequence of the parallel constructions) that this quatrain, unlike the other two, never comes to focus upon one of the temporal stages of lust but moves freely among all three, for this establishes a greater separation from the experience, which can now be assimilated, like a distant panorama, in all its parts. (The fact that one quatrain is devoted mainly to the "before" phase, and one to the "after", while the act itself is only touched on in passing, subtly reinforces the irony inherent in lust, the terrible disparity between the prolonged and intense emotional cost—both in the struggles to attain the object, and the subsequent shame and remorse—and the momentary spasm of pleasure that this pays for.) A similar effect of increasing distance and disengagement is produced by the sequence of epithets applied here to lust. In lines nine and ten the stages of lust are equated, first under the term "Mad" (brought over from the previous quatrain), then under the weaker "extreme". This diminuendo proceeds much further in the next two lines, where the stages are contrasted: "A bliss" asserts the most favorable view of lust we have yet seen, even through it is partly canceled out by "a very woe"; and finally, "a joy" is much less seriously qualified by "a dream", a surprisingly mild negation which does not point to anything evil or even unpleasant in lust, but only to the transient nature of its satisfactions, and which leaves us with the impression (enforced by its crucial position as the last word before the couplet) that the entire disturbing experience is now fading out in the speaker's memory and is beginning to take on, along with the painful remorse that it at first evoked, a vague air of unreality.

The two epithets of the couplet confirm this impression. It is true that "this hell" is the most condemnatory term in the entire poem, and its position at the end gives it greater weight than "dream"; but it is undercut in advance by "heaven", the most commendatory term (which exactly balances "hell" and is equally remote from the actual physical event that precipitated all this), as well as by the tone of weary hopelessness that pervades the couplet, showing the final exhaustion of the speaker's energies. This couplet is not a conclusion, in the sense of a logical consequence or summary or application of what was said in the quatrains, which might trouble those who view the poem as a form of statement. If, however, one regards the poem as an attempt to dramatize the internal "action" that the speaker is undergoing, then this couplet becomes understandable as the denouement to that action—indeed, to borrow from Aristotle's dramatic terminology, it is an "unexpected but probable" denouement, which he argues is the best type. It is unexpected since the ideas and feelings expressed in the opening lines would lead us to predict that the speaker (if not all the world) would henceforward know well to shun this heaven; but upon looking back we realize that this change in attitude, like the peripety of a well-constructed plot, has been carefully prepared for by the development up to this point, by the gradual dissipation of the man's disgust in the body of the sonnet. This dissipation has itself been made probable, both on general psychological grounds—as what might be expected when anyone has freely given vent to his painful emotions, and their immediate cause has receded into the background—and also in terms of the specific situation here, the insidious power of sexual desire and the speaker's weakness with respect to it. We never learn a great deal about the speaker, but we can infer enough to comprehend this action, for he is not meant to be highly individualized or unusual in this aspect of his character. It is clear, for instance, that this is not the first time he has experienced lust and its bitter aftermath, though experience evidently has not prevented a repetition of the cycle. It is also very significant that he never explicitly directs his anger at himself for succumbing, but throughout displaces it on the abstraction "lust", and so manages to avoid acknowledging his own responsibility. The couplet only continues this process a step further, since it is really a form of rationalization both before and after the fact—a way of assuaging his guilt over his past action by convincing himself that he is no worse than everyone else, and of establishing in advance an excuse for surrendering anew to the same temptation. For the basic irony of the poem, it seems to me, is this dramatic demonstration that in this man (part of whom we must recognize in ourselves) the revulsion that lust always produces cannot long hold out against the pleasure that lust always promises. After the act of lust, he realized, in his disgust, that it was an expense of spirit, but this poem (or, rather, the action that it renders) has been an expense of his disgust, and so there is now nothing more to keep this "after" stage from fading into the next "before" stage.

It is this complex reversal that most clearly distinguishes Sonnet CXXIX from the two poems with which it is most frequently compared, Sidney's "Thou blind man's mark, thou fool's self-chosen snare" and Donne's "Farewell to love", for although both of these deal with the same subject, their treatment of it is essentially static (in that the speaker himself is not undergoing an experience in the poem, but is only developing a conclusion he has already reached). It also distinguishes the sonnet from the parallels usually cited in Shakespeare's own work, the passages on lust in *The Rape of Lucrece*, ll. 687–742, *Hamlet* I. v. 55–57, *Measure for Measure* I. ii. 131–134, etc. It is easy to see why those who regard this poem as a statement about lust should have sought parallels in terms of mere similarity of mere subject matter; but if one looks instead for the portrayal of a similar psychological evolution, then I think an interesting comparison can be made with Hamlet's third soliloquy (II. ii. 575–633). I know of nothing in Shakespeare that comes closer to the crucial third and fourth lines of this sonnet than Hamlet's

> Bloody, bawdy villain!
> Remorseless, treacherous, lecherous, kindless villain!

The subject is entirely different, of course, but the same sort of emotional crisis is being represented. Hamlet, like the speaker in the sonnet, is overcome with bitter disgust at his past action (or rather, inaction), and at the climax of excitement his syntax breaks down into this violent outburst of disjointed exclamations. But while this barrage of abuse marks the high point of his anger, it also, as in the sonnet, shows his impotence, for it is nothing more than a kind of futile name-calling that he must substitute for meaningful action. Moreover, Hamlet, too, has managed to displace his anger from its real object, which is himself, to an external object that he has failed to oppose. (In the soliloquy this is much more obvious than in the sonnet, since we can actually follow the course of this displacement: Hamlet begins by castigating himself, and the very epithets—"slave" and "villain"—that he originally applied to himself are later transferred to the King.) The final and I think most revealing similarity between the two speeches lies in their consequences, for they both become vehicles of catharsis, enabling each speaker, through the process of displacement and of verbal attack upon the surrogate "enemy", to discharge his guilt and so arrive at a resolution of his painful situation—a resolution which is transient and ineffectual, but which brings him some solace. Hamlet travels much farther along this road than does the speaker of the sonnet, ending on a note not of resignation but of apparent triumph as he gets caught up in his scheme to test the Ghost's word, which at the beginning of the soliloquy he believed implicitly (an abrupt change that I suspect can be explained more satisfac-torily by this mode of psychological analysis than by any amount of research into Elizabethan attitudes toward ghosts). And he is at least at one point aware of what he is doing. But what he says of himself then is equally true of the speaker of the sonnet, who has also, like a whore, unpacked his heart with words, and so unwittingly betrayed his original impulse. This speaker, who is necessarily (given the brevity of the sonnet form) so much less complex and individuated than Hamlet, never quite realizes the irony inherent in his verbalization of his self-disgust, but Shakespeare has built it into the very structure of this poignant, fourteen-line drama.

—Richard Levin, "Sonnet CXXIX as a 'Dramatic' Poem." *Shakespeare Quarterly* 16 (1965): p. 179.

ᘒ

Thomas M. Greene on "The Expence of Spirit" and Social Class

[Thomas M. Greene is Professor of English and Comparative Lit-erature at Yale University. His books include *Descent from Heaven: The Study of Epic Calamity, Rabelais: A Study of Comic Courage, Ben Johnson and the Centered Self,* and *The Light in Troy: Imitation and Discovery in Renaissance,* and *The Vulnerable Text,* a book of essays.

In Sonnet 129 the opening phrase immediately presents a kind of hermeneutic hurdle. The expression "expence of Spirit" sustains the funda-mental metaphor of the sequence linking economics with emotion and sex-uality. The constant concern with husbandry, with cost-accounting, with thrift and profligacy, with a friendship too dear for one's possessing, with bonds and terms and leases—this repetitive series of analogies organizes the *Sonnets,* and there is nothing a priori in this figural pattern that is neces-sarily inaccessible to a twentieth-century reader. The metaphor begins to lose us only when the economic implications of "expence" are taken literally at the physiological level. The sexual act is really impoverishing only if one holds the medieval and Renaissance belief that it shortens a man's life. If, in place of the restorative, therapeutic release our post-Freudian society per-ceives, one attributed to sex a literal expenditure of vitality, then the struggle between the sexes takes on a crude economic reality, and we begin to understand the linkage made by the Wyf of Bath. She ends her tale by praying for "housebondes meeke, yonge, and fressh abedde" while calling down a plague on "olde and angry niggardes of dispence." In Sonnets 1–126 of Shakespeare's sequence, the bourgeois poet speaks for the values of hus-bandry, as befits his class, in order prudently to correct the failures of this art assigned to that social class of "unthrifts" which includes the friend. It is true that the conduct associated with good husbandry shifts radically; if in Sonnets 1–17 it means marriage, and solitude is "unprovident," by Sonnet 95 ("They that haue powre to hurt . . .") only the solitary can "husband natures ritches from expence," with a stinginess not calculated to please the

Wyf of Bath. In Sonnet 129 the young man's profligacy is less at issue than, one presumes, the bourgeois speaker's among others. The phrase "th'ex-pence of Spirit" means several things, including the implication that the speaker has been *unclassed* by lust, that he is now guilty of that aristocratic waste he had attempted in so many preceding poems to moderate. In yielding to lust he is yielding to a literally self-destructive extravagance, which heretofore he has followed tradition in charging to his social superiors. This biological as well as sociological undoing of the self, implicit in Shakespeare's word "expence," remains an abstraction for us even if we catch its resonance. We might begin to recapture that reference to personal ontology by taking seriously the lost implications of such words as "dissolute" and "dissipated."

> —Thomas M. Greene, "Anti-hermeneutics: The Case of Shakespeare's Sonnet 129." In *Poetic Traditions of the English Renaissance*, ed. Maynard Mack and George deForest Lord. (New Haven, CT: Yale University Press, 1982), pp. 147–148.

⊗

JOEL FINEMAN ON THE PARADOX OF PRAISE IN THE DARK LADY SONNETS

[Joel Fineman, Professor of English Literature at the University of California at Berkeley, is the author of *Shakespeare's Perjured Eye* (1986) and *The Subjectivity Effect in Western Literary Tradition* (1991). Fineman accepts the traditional division of the sonnets: 1–126 addressed to a young man, and 127–154 addressed to the dark lady. He argues that in the Sonnets, Shakespeare creates a new poetic subjectivity, a new poetics and a new first-person. The Sonnets also become a point of departure for thoughts about gender, and the nature of modern subjectivity.]

Where the first sub-sequence consistently presents the young man as the mirror image of his poet's ideal praise, the second sub-sequence instead develops the dark lady as the speaking figure of her poet's speech, not the visual but the verbal instantiation of what her poet says about her. Where the young man is the picture of his poet's admiration—one that leaves the poet at a loss for words: "my dumb thoughts, speaking in effect"—the dark lady is instead the *discourse* of her poet's lust, as though it were language itself that is responsible for lasciviously fleshing out the poet's first suspicions of poetic ornament, as in sonnet 147:

> My thoughts and my discourse as madmen's are,
> At random from the truth vainly express'd;
> For I have sworn the fair, and thought thee bright,
> Who art as black as hell, as dark as night.

This progress, from an uncertainly ascetic poetry of picture to a definitively erotic poetry of word, from a vestigially ideal poetics of *ut pictura poesis* to, as it were, a sexy and unhappy poetics of *ut poesis poesis*, represents in very obvious ways a fundamental rewriting of the assumptions of the poetry of praise, not least of those assumptions that such poetry makes about itself. Acting out what seems to be a preordained conclusion, the poet's praise becomes its own rebuke when it is distanced from its ideal image of itself, just as all the poet's old poetic gold loses its currency when it is reassessed and seen to be a counterfeit. Moreover, according to the poet, it is these specifically epidiectic disappointments that make of admiration an "expense of spirit in a waste of shame." Again we come upon the fact that the relationship of the first sub-sequence to the second is neither one of simple repetition nor of simple contrast. As Romeo says:

> These happy masks that kiss fair ladies' brows,
> Being black, puts us in mind they hide the fair,
> He that is strooken blind cannot forget
> The precious treasure of his eyesight lost.
> (Romeo and Juliet I.i. 230–233)

The darkness of the second sub-sequence is just such a reminding and memorializing mask, a masquerading blackness that, "being black," explicitly recalls the fairness that it hides. Built up on and as the ruin of the first, the second sub-sequence is both cause and consequence of visionary blindness. Even so, it still presents itself as the true record of the way that it is blind.

This seems the most striking aspect of the dark lady sonnets, the way they both mask and unmask a fairness they in this way both cover and discover, the way they come, like Antony, to bury and to praise a Caesar over whose dead body they mournfully, duplicitously, and yet, like Antony, still honestly discourse. For if the dark lady sonnets speak against the visionary truth of a traditional poetic speech, this loss of an ideal veracity, both poetic and erotic, is at the same time the one regret, both poetic and erotic, that the paradox of praise can say it speaks with perfect truth. As we will see, it is in a very coherent way that the paradox of praise, which is traditionally a device of comic and rhetorical play, a way of not really saying what one really means, becomes in the dark lady sub-sequence something that takes itself, and thereby forces its readers to take it, both more seriously and more literally than the ironic young man sonnets take the idealizing tradition of the poetry of praise. The dark lady sonnets articulate directly what the young man sonnets only gesture at obliquely. But this explication of the young man sonnets' implications enforces a poetic consequence that the young man sonnets do not, and this because, activating the poetics of the paradox of praise, *performing* the belying that they speak about, the dark lady sonnets actually and literally *speak* a double truth that, no longer "constant" to "one thing expressing," admits itself to be a "lie":

> Thou blind fool, Love, what dost thou to mine eyes,
> That they behold and see not what they see?
> They know what beauty is, see where it lies,
> Yet what the best is take the worst to be.

—Joel Fineman, *Shakespeare's Perjured Eye*. (Berkeley: University of California Press, 1986), p. 160–162. ⦿

Summary Analysis of
"The Phoenix and Turtle"

This 67-line poem appeared in 1601. The poem celebrates love's ability to turn striking differences into complementarity. Specifically, the marriage of the phoenix and the turtledove is held up as an example of ideal love in the face of individual differences. The phoenix is famous for her beauty; the turtledove for his constancy in love. Together, they lived as one:

> Hearts remote yet not asunder,
> Distance and no space was seen
> 'Twixt this turtle and his queen.
> But in them it were a wonder.
>
> (29–32)

"The Phoenix and Turtle" is written in 13 quatrains with rhyme scheme abba followed by a threnos consisting of five rhymed triplets. Thematically, the poem can be divided into three sections: the calling together of a funeral procession of birds (1–20), the anthem sung by the mourners (21–52), and the threnos, or lament for the dead (53–67). Reason, the lyrics of the anthem tell us, was "confounded" (41) by the complete and binding love between two such seemingly mismatched birds. Reason's wonder moved it to create the threnos as a tribute to the phoenix and the turtledove.

Many critics have discussed the difficulties of interpreting "The Phoenix and Turtle." It has been said that the lines of the poem present one of the most difficult problems to be found in Shakespeare's work (Newdigate), and that the composition of the poem is unique in European literature (Shahani). Some critics concentrate on the poem's possible external references to real people and situations, whereas others discuss the metaphysical ideas behind the poem's anthem. ❀

Critical Views on
"The Phoenix and Turtle"

RONALD BATES ON PAST CRITICAL ERRORS IN ANALYZING
THE POEM

[In this extract, Ronald Bates discusses what he considers the
"errors" in previous critics' attempts to analyze "The Phoenix and
Turtle," addressing questions of the identity of various symbols
within the poem.]

There are few English poems more enigmatic than Shakespeare's "The
Phoenix and Turtle". This fact, obvious from a single reading, is further
emphasized by the relative paucity of studies devoted to its elucidation. Moreover, a good deal of the criticism has been concentrated on the more external
aspects; the occasion of the work and the actual persons symbolized by the
Phoenix and Turtle have so taken up scholarly interest as to leave the poem
itself a relative mystery. Yet, even if it could be proved beyond a doubt that the
Phoenix was meant to "shadow forth", say, Lady Bedford, this historical fact
would not in any aesthetically satisfactory way elucidate the main problem:
the particular poem by Shakespeare and its particular effect on the reader. In
this essay I do not claim to have completely solved the problem, but by a
closer attention to the poem, in relation to Shakespeare's work as a whole, I
have attempted to clear up some previous critical errors—for example, the
identity of "the bird of loudest lay"—and to indicate certain relations with his
other works that may help us to understand to some degree Shakespeare's
strange and unique tone in "The Phoenix and Turtle".

To begin with, the poem is divided into three quite distinct sections: the
funeral party (stanzas 1–5), the anthem (stanzas 6–13), and the threnos
(stanzas 14–18). The reader's problems begin at once with the first section.
Which is "the bird of loudest lay" is a question to which various answers
have been given, none very satisfactory. Grosart, for instance, suggested the
nightingale, although his remark that other critics might have other choices
seems to imply some doubt on his own part. Shahani and Bonnard, however, accept the nightingale with no apparent hesitation. Fairchild, leaning
too heavily on his hypothesis that Shakespeare drew on *The Parlement of
Foules* for the first five stanzas, came to the conclusion that the bird must be
the crane, "the geaunt, with his trompes soune", as Chaucer described him.
Basically, two methods of analysis are represented by all this, if we consider
the text as the central point. Grosart examines stanza one, with its key
descriptive words, "loudest lay", "herald", "trumpet", and "chaste wings", and
then considers what bird these words suggest to him. He relies greatly on
"chaste wings", which, for him, give a wonderfully accurate picture of the
nightingale in flight. (That he is confused here is obvious. The "chaste
wings" do not belong to "the bird of loudest lay", but are obedient to it.)
Fairchild examines the same stanza, and the same key words, and then, on
the sole basis of what another poet has written in one other poem—with
the consequent reliance, in this case, on "trumpet"—gets an entirely different bird to fill the role. There seems to me to be only one alternative,

especially after A.E. Armstrong, in *Shakespeare's Imagery*, has shown what can be learned about Shakespeare's use of language. Let us examine the words in "The Phoenix and Turtle", not merely in relation to our reaction to them, or Chaucer's use of them, but in light of how Shakespeare uses them at other times.

—Ronald Bates, "Shakespeare's 'The Phoenix and Turtle.'" In *Shakespeare Quarterly* 66, (1955), pp. 19–20.

G. WILSON KNIGHT ON THE BIRDS' RESPECTIVE GENDERS

[G. Wilson Knight (1897–1985), a leading British Shakespeare scholar, taught drama and English literature at the University of Leeds. He was the author of many volumes of criticism, including *The Wheel of Fire* (1930), *The Starlit Dome* (1941), *The Crown of Life* (1947), and *Shakespeare and Religion* (1967). This extract was taken from his book *The Mutual Flame* (1955).]

We have already equated the Turtle, or Turtle-Dove, with the female element in the Shakespearian bisexuality which loved the Fair Youth and composed the plays. The Turtle-Dove is a normal Shakespearian symbol of love-constancy, as at *I Henry VI*, II, ii, 30–1. The dove is Venus' bird: her car is drawn by 'two strengthless doves' at *Venus and Adonis*, 153; the association recurs elsewhere (e.g. *The Rape of Lucrece*, 58; *Romeo and Juliet*, II, v, 7); and in *The Tempest* (IV, i, 94) Venus' dove is associated directly with her island, Paphos, as in *Love's Martyr*. We should normally in Shakespeare expect a single Turtle-Dove to be female, as in Paulina's lines:

> I, an old turtle,
> Will wing me to some wither'd bough, and there
> My mate, that's never to be found again,
> Lament till I am lost.
> (*The Winter's Tale*, V, iii, 132)

The bird itself is female even when compared with a male, as when Troilus insists that he is as true 'as turtle to her mate' (*Troilus and Cressida*, III, ii, 185). But here, on the pattern of our other poems, the Turtle is the male partner. That this is not quite natural within Shakespeare's world may be seen from the equation of the dove with gentleness underlying Juliet's agonised, 'Dove-feather'd raven! wolvish-ravening lamb!' (*Romeo and Juliet*, III, ii, 76); and, still more, by the series of paradoxes developed by Helena in *A Midsummer Night's Dream* when, with a significant grouping of effects, she compares herself ironically to Daphne chasing Apollo, the dove pursuing a griffin, or a 'mild hind' the tiger (II, i, 231–3). We do not expect our Turtle to be, in any obvious sense, a typical male: that is certain.

As for the Phoenix, it is always, and necessarily, baffling. It occurs in the Sonnets:

> Devouring time, blunt thou the lion's paws,
> And make the earth devour her own sweet brood;
> Pluck the keen teeth from the fierce tiger's jaws,
> And burn the long-liv'd Phoenix in her blood . . .
>
> (19)

Lion and tiger are natural associations, and we must never forget that it is itself a kind of eagle. It is pre-eminently royal and golden, whereas the Dove is 'silver' (*Venus and Adonis*, 366, 1190). In *A Lover's Complaint*, the 'beauteous' and 'maiden-tongued' (99–100) youth, who so resembles the young man of the Sonnets, is given a phoenix-comparison:

> Small show of man was yet upon his chin;
> His phoenix down began but to appear
> Like unshorn velvet on that termless skin,
> Whose bare out-bragg'd the web it seem'd to wear;
> Yet show'd his visage by that cost more dear,
> And nice affections wavering stood in doubt
> If best were as it was, or best without.
>
> (92)

The Phoenix is used here more naturally for the borderline, and so in a sense bisexual, age of the youth, set between boyhood and manhood, and we may observe how precisely this border-line state of 'down' is, as in the Sonnets, shown as the secret of the attraction, and how exactly it is related to the Phoenix. But the Phoenix may also be a creature of militant virility, as in 3 *Henry VI*:

> YORK: My ashes, as the Phoenix, may bring forth
> A bird that will revenge upon you all,
> And in that hope I throw mine eyes to heaven
> Scorning whate'er you can afflict me with.
> Why come you not? what! multitudes, and fear?
> CLIFFORD: So cowards fight when they can fly no further;
> So doves do peck the falcon's piercing talons;
> So desperate thieves, all hopeless of their lives,
> Breathe out invectives 'gainst the officers.
>
> (I, iv, 35)

Compare Enobarbus' 'In that mood, the dove will peck the estridge' (*Antony and Cleopatra*, III, xi, 195). The Phoenix is associated with strong action, backed by 'heaven'; the Dove with female weakness, in contrast to the falcon's 'talons'. Traditionally the Phoenix is represented as an eagle-like bird, with just such talons of its own.

In *Richard III* the Phoenix' 'nest of spicery' is once compared by Richard to natural procreation, with the womb as both the grave of old bitterness and the nurture-ground of comfort (IV, iv, 424). The context is dramatically ironical.

Shakespeare's two most resplendent male lovers, Timon and Antony, are compared with it. Timon, who 'flashes now a Phoenix' (II, i, 32), enjoys the comparison the more appropriately in that his love and personality are abnormal: he has, in fact, precisely those magical qualities, that blend of sweetness with virility, that lonely completion, which the bird symbolises. The comparison of Antony to 'thou Arabian Bird' (*Antony and Cleopatra*, III, ii, 12), humorously reported as coming from Lepidus, is relevant, though less important.

Female and royal persons of chastity and virtue may also receive the comparison. Imogen, with her 'mind so rare', is 'alone the Arabian bird' (*Cymbeline*, I, vi, 17); and in Cranmer's prophecy at the conclusion to *Henry VIII*, Queen Elizabeth is compared to 'the bird of wonder' or 'maiden Phoenix', from 'the sacred ashes' of whose 'honour'—it is a *spiritual* propagation—a new sovereign is to rise in 'star-like' majesty (*Henry VIII*, V, v, 40–8).

The bird can be crisply defined as a character of the highest virtue, in both the old and the modern senses of the word. It holds magical properties; power must be contained; and it is significant that our two female candidates are royal. Its presence in *The Tempest* is natural:

> Now I will believe
> That there are unicorns; that in Arabia
> There is one tree, the Phoenix' throne, one Phoenix
> At this hour reigning there.
>
> (III, iii, 21)

Observe the 'throne': it is a royal bird, a kind of super-eagle.

—G. Wilson Knight, *The Mutual Flame*. (London: Methuen & Co. Ltd., 1955), pp. 195–198.

⊗

Murray Copland on "The Phoenix and Turtle" and Platonism

[In this essay, Murray Copland makes the case that "The Phoenix and Turtle" is an expression of Platonic philosophy, and discusses the symbolism of the conjunction of the two birds.]

Countless writers, even Wilson Knight among them, have committed the howler—for surely it is that—of referring to Shakespeare's poem as "The Phoenix and the Turtle". If, in Platonic terms, the Phoenix represents the 'idea' of female beauty and the Turtle the 'idea' of fidelity, mated they have grown into a third 'idea' which by virtue of its ideality will necessarily have to include these two. This is, of course, the 'idea' of human love—human love in its barely imaginable perfection. Now I take it that an 'idea' cannot be a duality; it must be a unity. Shakespeare appears to have called his poem *The Phoenix and Turtle*. That is, the subject is one thing, not two.

In the line

> *Phoenix* and the *Turtle* fled,

they *are* presented as separate creatures, but only in aid of the next antithetical line wherein they are all the more strikingly fused:

> In a mutuall flame from hence.

Here *Phoenix* needs no article, precisely because of the bird's uniqueness: whereas *Turtle* needs its 'the' to establish (for this is the first mention of the dead protagonists) that this is not any old turtle (as, in fact, is the case in *Love's Martyr*) but itself a type, an ideal, and therefore unique, just as much as its mate.

It is immaterial whether Shakespeare had two actual dead lovers in mind. But I do not think the poem is being properly read if the reader does not realise that human love is under discussion; he should appreciate that behind the birds an eminently desirable human possibility is being mooted. If such a man and woman could exist and love like this, then *The Phoenix and Turtle* would be their fitting elegy.

It may be clear by now that I am against overmuch mystifying of this poem, which critics have tended to etherealise out of existence.

Is it so very crude to see in Shakespeare's acceptance of Chester's bright idea of a mated Phoenix a rather original, compellingly beautiful, but nonetheless natural and likely enough conceit to come upon in a late-Elizabethan Platonizing poem? Donne himself filched the idea of his own "Parliament of Fowls" poem, the delightful St. Valentine's Day Epithalamion, where the application is wholly unmysterious and as 'human' as could be—an actual wedding:

> Till now, Thou warmd'st with multiplying loves
> Two larkes, two sparrows, or two Doves,
>   All that is nothing unto this,
> For thou this day couplest two Phoenixes.

But Donne is not here in a particularly 'Platonic' vein; that would scarcely suit his occasion:

> . . . one bed containes, through Thee,
> Two Phoenixes, whose joyned breasts
> Are unto one another mutuall nests,
> Where motion kindles such fires, as shall give
> Young Phoenixes, and yet the old shall live.

The Elizabethans, sexually, must have been on the whole a happily proficient, promiscuous, and uninhibited race. We can assume this from the fascinated glee with which they pounced upon the newly unearthed Platonic version of love and made it all the fashionable rage. Lord Herbert of Cherbury's serious-minded Melander and Celinda are happily conscious of their limelighted position as, in Gilbert's phrase, 'most particularly pure' young people. It is their sense of the wild eccentricity of the notion which causes these poets to place such stress on the abstention from physical intercourse. The exaggerated contempt in which they place bodily pleasure has little to do with Plato, who notably conveys an appreciation of its charms.

The Shakespeare stanza about 'married Chastitie' comes as a shock because Shakespeare meant it to do so. Poems in the 'metaphysical' mode characteristically proceed by shock tactics, both of style and of thought. *The Phoenix and Turtle* is very obviously a single, somewhat haughtily restrained demonstration on Shakespeare's part that if 'everyone was doing it, doing it, doing it' he was very well competent to do it too; and, by a natural enough impulse under the circumstances, there is perhaps present a certain willingness to outdo all the others in sheer transcendence of transcendentalism.

—Murray Copland, "The Dead Phoenix." In *Essays in Criticism* 15 (1965), pp. 279–281.

Summary Analysis of
The Rape of Lucrece

The Rape of Lucrece was entered on the Stationers' Register on May 9, 1594, under the title *The Ravyshement of Lucrece*. Perhaps *The Rape of Lucrece* was the poem of "graver labour" that Shakespeare spoke of in his dedication of *Venus and Adonis* to the Earl of Southampton. Shakespeare also dedicated *The Rape of Lucrece* to him. This dedication, however, has a much more intimate tone than the previous one: "The love I dedicate to your Lordship is without end," it begins. *The Rape of Lucrece* went through six editions during Shakespeare's lifetime; eight more were published by 1640. Shakespeare's contemporaries also frequently quoted the poem.

It is generally agreed that the genre of *The Rape of Lucrece* is complaint, a form that was especially popular in the late 1590s. Complaints focus on the suffering of their protagonists, who are powerless to change the present or the future. Like Samuel Daniel, who published a poem called *The Complaint of Rosamond* in 1592, Shakespeare used the rhyme royal (a seven-line stanza in iambic pentameter with rhyme scheme ababbcc) in writing his complaint poem.

The plot for this erotic narrative poem is derived from Livy's history of Rome, Ovid's *Fasti*, and maybe, as some critics argue, from Chaucer's *Legend of Good Women* and William Painter's *Palace of Pleasure*.

In this "pamphlet without beginning" as Shakespeare describes it in his dedication, we are plunged into the poem's main conflict. Because Collatine praises the virtue of his beautiful young wife, Lucrece, his friend Tarquin's passion is aroused. From the first stanza we learn that Tarquin is leaving besieged Ardea, located twenty-four miles south of Rome, to go to Collatium. Bearing the "lightless fire" (4) of lust in his heart, he is going there to seduce Lucrece. Lucrece graciously welcomes him as one of Collatine's friends. As Tarquin lies awake that night, he is torn between his desire for Lucrece and his dread of the consequences of taking her and being caught. The narrator gives us an exquisite digression about greed at this point:

> So that in vent'ring ill we leave to be
> The things we are, for that which we expect;
> And this ambitious foul infirmity,
> In having much, torments us with defect
> Of what we have: so then we do neglect
>   The thing we have, and all for want of wit,
>   Make something nothing by augmenting it.
>   (148–154)

Shakespeare reveals Tarquin's conflicted state of mind. The valiant warrior rebukes himself for his weakness, and his rational mind frankly assesses the situation:

> What win I if I gain the thing I seek?
> A dream, a breath, a froth of fleeting joy.

Who buys a minute's mirth to wail a week,
Or sells eternity to get a toy?

(211–214)

But Tarquin's armor of reason fails him. He takes up the torch that will light his way to Lucrece's room. The locks on the door to her chamber have to be forced open, the wind almost blows out his torch, he pricks his finger on Lucrece's needle—but none of these "forbiddings" (323) can stop him. Desire is his pilot; beauty, his prize.

Once inside Lucrece's room, he gazes down upon her as she sleeps in her "yet-unstained bed" (366). Tarquin places his hand upon her breast ("Her breasts like ivory globe circled with blue,/A pair of maiden worlds unconquered;" [407–408]). Lucrece wakes up trembling with terror. He tells her that, despite the consequences, he must "enjoy" her, and that he will use force if necessary. If she submits, he promises to keep it a secret, rationalizing that "The fault unknown is as a thought unacted" (527). Lucrece tearfully pleads with Tarquin to spare her by virtue of his knighthood, his social standing, his friendship with her husband, by her tears, by holy human law, and even by heaven and earth, but he remains unmoved. He muffles her cries with the bedclothes as he violates her. Immediately after he completes the act, Tarquin's dire predictions of his downfall seem to begin coming true:

(Ev'n in this thought) through the dark night he stealeth,
A captive victor that hath lost in gain,
Bearing away the wound that nothing healeth,
The scar that will despite the cure remain;
Leaving his spoil perplex'd in greater pain:
    She bears the load of lust he left behind,
    And he the burden of a guilty mind.

(729–735)

Lucrece, instantly degraded into "a hopeless castaway" (743), beats her breast in anguish and launches into a lengthy lament. She repeatedly reaches the conclusion that she is irreparably ruined, and that her shame is public as well as private:

The nurse to still her child will tell my story,
And fright her crying babe with Tarquin's name.
The orator to deck his oratory
Will couple my reproach to Tarquin's shame.
Feast-finding minstrels tuning my defame
    Will tie the hearers to attend each line,
    How Tarquin wronged me, I Collatine.

(813–819)

Her desperate tirade against opportunity and time reinforces Lucrece's role as helpless victim:

In vain I rail at Opportunity,
At Time, at Tarquin, and uncheerful Night;

> In vain I cavil with mine infamy;
> In vain I spurn at my confirmed despite:
> This helpless smoke of words doth me no right.
> The remedy indeed to do me good
> Is to let forth my foul defiled blood.
>
> (1023–1029)

Despite her victimization, Lucrece, decides to become "the mistress of (her) fate" (1069) after all by taking her own life. But she will not die until Collatine learns the cause of her death—and vows to avenge her.

Day comes and Lucrece calls for her maid, who is moved to tears by the mere sight of her mistress. Lucrece feels unable to divulge the cause of the "deep torture" (1287) in her heart, but she bids the maid to send a messenger to Collatine.

While she waits, she looks at a picture of the siege and fall of Troy in lines 1366–1561. In her grief, she identifies with the painted face of Hecuba watching her husband, King Priam of Troy, die. So profound is Lucrece's sense of suffering that she faults the picture's painter for failing to endow his image of Hecuba with the power to cry out: "And therefore Lucrece swears he did her wrong/ To give her so much grief, and not a tongue" (1462–1463). Such a detailed digression is a convention of the complaint genre. The passage also allows time to elapse until the messenger returns with Collatine. Shakespeare would refer to Hecuba's grief again in *Hamlet*.

When Collatine returns home and sees his Lucrece's sad face, he is initially unable to ask her what has happened. The narrator says that "Both stood like old acquaintance in a trance,/ Met far from home, wond'ring each other's chance" (1595–1596). Finally, he inquires. Lucrece is too devastated to reply at once: "Three times with sighs she gives her sorrow fire/ Ere once she can discharge one word of woe" (1604–1605). She tells him of her shame without naming the culprit. When Collatine demands his name, Lucrece asks the assembled soldiers to promise that her honor will be avenged before revealing her attacker. After naming Tarquin, she stabs herself.

Collatine stands "stone-still" (1730), while his wife's father, Lucretius, throws himself down on her body. Collatine snaps out of his daze and does the same. He "counterfeits" (1776) to die with Lucrece, but his friend Brutus stops him. "Is it revenge to give thyself a blow/ For this foul act by whom thy fair wife bleeds?" he asks Collatine (1823–1824). Brutus counsels him to seek revenge for for Lucrece's death in the name of Rome and her chaste soul. The body of Lucrece is carried through Rome in order to "publish Tarquin's foul offense" (1852). Tarquin is banished from Rome in short order.

As F. T. Prince points out, *Venus and Adonis* is more in keeping with the spirit of comedy; *The Rape of Lucrece,* with the spirit of tragedy. Shakespeare explores the unstoppable self-destructiveness of Tarquin and the bottomless grief of Lucrece far more deeply than he does the psyches of either Venus or Adonis. We can trace from this poem the development not only of Shakespeare's imagery, but also of his compelling depictions of the mental states of the protagonists in his later works. ❀

Critical Views on
The Rape of Lucrece

RICHARD LANHAM ON THE IMPORTANCE OF LANGUAGE
OVER PASSION IN THE POEM

[Richard Lanham, Professor of English at the University of California in Los Angeles, is the author of *Sidney's Old Arcadia, Handlist of Rhetorical Terms, Tristram Shandy: The Games of Pleasure, Revising Prose,* and *Analyzing Prose.* He is also the author of *The Motives of Eloquence: Literary Rhetoric in the Renaissance* (1976), from which this extract is taken.]

If we think the poem about sexual passion, we shall again collapse into laughter at the absurd language. Tarquin puts his hand on Lucrece's breast much as Napoleon must have pointed to Russia on the map. The language makes sense only if rhetoric, and more especially feudal rhetoric, is the subject of the poem. Tarquin finally tells Lucrece that because "nothing can affection's course control" he must "embrace mine infamy." The force *we* have seen in this poem is not affection but language, and he is doomed to embrace his own infamy because it has been with him all the time.

The poem has become, by this point, clearly a study in dramatic motive. It should not surprise us, therefore, that Tarquin's attempt to persuade Lucrece, and her reply, are both developed within a rhetorical reality. He argues, "The fault unknown is as a thought unacted." A feudal threat again, nameless bastardy: "Bequeath not to their lot / The shame that from them no device can take." It is the heraldic term he thinks of—"device." Lucrece replies that he has changed roles: "In Tarquin's likeness I did entertain thee. / Hast thou put on his shape to do him shame?" (ll. 596–97). He is not acting the king, she tells him at length, concluding again with a theatrical metaphor: "Think but how vile a spectacle it were / To view thy present trespass in another" (ll. 631–32). And, after only a few dozen lines more, he steps on the torch and, between lines 686 and 687, does the deed. The poem never describes it. Shakespeare stresses again that his subject is motive, not sexual passion, not an act but the psychic superstructure built upon it. Tarquin then slinks off in shame, the narrator comparing, in a complex figure (l. 715 ff.), *his hero's* state of mind to a besieged temple, his soul the doyenne thereof.

Compare Tarquin's "desire" with Venus's in *Venus and Adonis,* and you see how complex a portrait Tarquin's is and how utterly asexual his passion. He falls in love with feudal rhetoric, not a woman; falls, in an odd but real way, in love with himself. His "lust" springs from his imagination as spontaneously as evil from the brain of Iago and for much the same reasons. Shakespeare begins with an undeniably serious motive and finds it, on analysis, more rhetorical even than Venus's substantial hunger.

The original title page of the poem, which read simply *Lucrece,* suggests that the poem explores less the rape than the Lucrece her rape reveals. She begins her self-revelation in a curious image: "She wakes her heart by beating on her breast" (l. 759), the first in a series of images which suggest self-exacerbated sorrow. Not one to "cloak offenses with a cunning brow," she wants night to stay forever. Then she excoriates it in a full-dress apostrophe, "O comfort-killing Night" (l. 763 ff.), which reveals the voice of outraged virtue resonating in a chamber of ego. Space and time must be annihilated to cover her disgrace: "O hateful, vaporous, and foggy Night, / . . . Make war against proportioned course of time" (l. 771, 774). The moon and stars must be ravished to keep her company: "Were Tarquin Night, as he is but Night's child, / The silver-shining queen he would distain; / her twinkling handmaids too, by him defiled, / . . . So should I have co-partners in my pain" (ll. 785–87, 789). She again thinks of her face as a mask, her predicament as a story:

> Make me not object to the telltale Day.
> The light will show, charactered in my brow,
> The story of sweet chastity's decay,
> The impious breach of holy wedlock vow.
> Yea, the illiterate, that know not how
> > To cipher what is writ in learnèd books,
> > Will quote my loathsome trespass in my looks.
>
> The nurse, to still her child, will tell my story
> And fright her crying babe with Tarquin's name.
> The orator, to deck his oratory,
> Will couple my reproach to Tarquin's shame.
> Feast-finding minstrels, tuning my defame,
> > Will tie the hearers to attend each line,
> > How Tarquin wrongèd me, I Collatine.
> > > [ll. 806–19]

We step back not simply from her echoing ego but from what she says. How has she wronged Collatine? She puts the problem in terms of feudal possession: "O unseen shame, invisible disgrace! / O unfelt sore, crest-wounding private scar!" (ll. 827–28). The excursus on the instability of possessions (l. 855 ff.) intensifies the question. Is sexual chastity, or honor, adequately described by the feudal cluster of metaphors? They describe a surface, a crest. And she is again vexed that her predicament is not *social*. To make the sin real, she has to confess it. This poem grows from a *demande*, of course, but as with Tarquin, the emphasis shifts: not, "Should she have given in?" but "Should she confess or shut up?" Lucrece herself cannot pose the problem so clearly. Carried away by her own eloquence, she bursts into an apostrophe to Opportunity. Absurd enough applied to Tarquin, as she does—he has *seized* his opportunity—it finds its real relevance applied to her, seizing the occasion to enjoy a good rant. The compulsive anaphora— one stanza begins uniformly with *Thou*, the next with *Thy* (l. 883 ff.), seventeen lines in three stanzas (l. 940 ff.) with *To*—tips the rhetorical explosion into something like comedy. She so obviously *enjoys* unpacking her heart with words. The poem acknowledges our suspicions openly at the end of the rant. She explodes with "Out, idle words, servants to shallow fools," and the reader returns a prompt "Just so."

Shakespeare then increases the comic distance by making language yet more self-consciously the subject: "Unprofitable sounds, weak arbitrators! /

Busy yourselves in skill-contending schools; / Debate where leisure serves with full debaters; / . . . For me, I force not argument a straw" (ll. 1017-19, 1021). This is ridiculous and meant to seem so. And gets more so. After forcing the argument yet further, she plunges back into—*anaphora*!

> In vain I rail at Opportunity,
> At Time, at Tarquin, and uncheerful Night;
> In vain I cavil with mine infamy;
> In vain I spurn at my confirmed despite:
> This helpless smoke of words doth me no right.
>   The remedy indeed to do me good
>   Is to let forth my foul defilèd blood.
>
>   [ll. 1023–29]

The non sequitur of the couplet is magnificent: "Words fail me. I'll kill myself!" She vows "in vain" some more because, like Pyrocles in the *Old Arcadia,* at the crucial moment she can't find a knife. The language here is meant to be entirely opaque. The point depends on it—what use in fact she is putting words to, the process by which vanity translates sorrow into pleasure. She is confused. She has lost her role. "Of that true type hath Tarquin rifled me." She is hammering out a new one—martyr of chastity. The logic of such a role is laughable but the language doesn't speak as the voice of logic, it speaks as the voice of ego, of identity trying to reconstitute itself.

—Richard Lanham, *The Motives of Eloquence: Literary Rhetoric in the Renaissance.* (New Haven, CT: Yale University Press, 1976), pp. 101–104.

℘

KATHERINE EISAMAN MAUS ON LANGUAGE AND ACCOUNTABILITY IN THE POEM

[In this essay, Katharine Eisaman Maus reads *The Rape of Lucrece* from a feminist perspective, discussing how language is used by the characters and the narrator both to obscure and expose the characters' accountability and motivations for their actions.]

What is happening when Tarquin compares himself to an army scaling Lucrece's fort, or when Lucrece imagines her body as a battered mansion? The usual assumption would be that these metaphors express states of mind. Both characters prefer metaphors which render their moral choices plausible. Thus Lucrece, who initially finds attractive the metaphor of the body and soul as "two babes" because the figure suggests the equality of body and soul, soon remarks that this metaphor makes her decision for suicide seem irrational. She answers her own objections by not confronting them directly, but by shifting to other, more congenial metaphors.

Nonetheless, the characters' rhetoric often seems as much constitutive as symptomatic, creating as well as expressing their states of mind. Tarquin's prosopopoeia, his personification of fears and desires and parts of the body as independent entities, is one indication of his moral disarray. But the trope also contributes to that disarray by implying that the personified impulses may take their own courses without reference to his intentions. Phrases like "my heart shall never countermand mine eye" or "affection is my captain, and he leadeth" suppress the fact of choice and allow Tarquin to avoid, at least temporarily, full recognition of his own culpability.

Lucrece's language similarly seems to determine the course of her reasoning. When Lucrece indicts Night, Opportunity, and Time after the rape, she employs both *prosopopoeia* and *metalepsis*, a rhetorical figure related to metaphor in which the remote is substituted for the obvious. Addressing "hateful, vaporous, and foggy Night," insisting that "thou art guilty of my cureless crime" (ll. 771–72), she simultaneously displaces responsibility from Tarquin and creates a plausible alternative culprit. By mystifying the fact of Tarquin's guilt, these tropes make it easier for Lucrece eventually to convict herself of a sin she has not committed.

In other ways, too, Lucrece's language persistently obscures the crucial question of agency: does the possessive pronoun in "my cureless crime" or "my life's foul deed" imply that she has committed an evil action or that an evil action has been committed against her? When she imagines that "The orator, to deck his oratory, / Will couple my reproach to Tarquin's shame" (ll. 815–16), is she using the word "reproach" to mean "complaint" or to mean "blameworthiness"? Her ambiguities have literally fatal consequences.

The problematic relationship between language and psychological state is suggested when Lucrece, after a night spent crying out against her wrong, sends a messenger to Collatine and must wait for his return. In the interval she finds herself frustrated and bored:

> The weary time she cannot entertain,
> For now 'tis stale to sigh, to weep and groan.
> So woe hath wearied woe, moan tirèd moan,
>   That she her plaints a little while doth stay,
>   Pausing for means to mourn some newer way.
>   (ll. 1361-65)

As Richard Lanham has noted, Lucrece's grief is not entirely spontaneous, but requires that she have something to say. She turns to a representation of the Trojan war for relief, not because it offers her the possibility of consolation, but because its novelty inspires her with new ways to describe and understand, and thus to experience her despair. This is not to say that discourse creates her grief. Her language is not prior to her psychological state in any simple way. Lucrece's model is Philomela, the raped bird-woman who not only suffers sexual outrage but who also makes it the constant subject of her utterance; and Lucrece remembers that in order to sing, Philomela must lean against a thorn, inflicting and re-inflicting Tereus's unwelcome penetration. The pain demands representation, but the representation requires the experience, even the deliberate exacerbation, of pain; the relation between emotion and speech seems more a perverse reciprocity than a simple relation of cause and effect. And it is a difficult cycle, constantly subject to disruption and blockage. Lucrece stutters when she attempts to plead with Tarquin, struggles through several drafts of her letter to Collatine, and stammers again when he finally arrives, interrupting both her story and her revelation of the culprit with "many accents and delays, / Untimely breathings, sick and short assays" (ll. 1719–20). Collatine likewise is struck mute upon his homecoming and babbles incoherently after Lucrece's suicide. On the one hand, grief and fear interrupt discourse, which inevitably seems an inadequate vehicle for feeling. On the other hand, grief and fear motivate discourse; Lucrece acquires her own voice in the poem only at the moment when she is faced with violence.

—Katharine Eisaman Maus, "Taking Tropes Seriously: Language and Violence in Shakespeare's *Rape of Lucrece*." In *Shakespeare Quarterly* 37 (1986): pp. 72–73.

HEATHER DUBROW ON THE POEM'S RHETORICAL AMBIGUITIES

[Heather Dubrow, Professor of English at Carleton College in Northfield, Minnesota, is the author of *Genre* (1982). She is also the author of *Captive Victors: Shakespeare's Narrative Poems and Sonnets* (1987), from which this extract is taken. Dubrow examines the connections between the sonnets and the narrative poems, pointing out that Shakespeare uses rhetoric to create characters as rich in complexities as those found in his dramatic works.]

Throughout *The Rape of Lucrece* Shakespeare manipulates our moral and emotional reactions to his personages. As in the case of *Venus and Adonis* (and, of course, Shakespeare's plays themselves), what we learn about the characters is intimately related to how we learn it. Our judgments of Tarquin are, of course, quite straightforward. In the case of Lucrece, however, our responses become more complex. On the one hand, by defining her own and her society's values as thoroughly as he does, Shakespeare makes clear how and why an event that would be traumatic for any victim is especially dreadful for her; our recognition that she is too innocent even to anticipate evil and the fact that her sense of self is based so totally on her chastity leads us to sympathize with her even more, a response that is heightened by our knowledge of how much her society itself valued that chastity. Yet, as we have seen, we are also very aware of the narrowness of vision symbolized by the fact that she focuses so much attention on Hecuba and so little on the other characters in the Troy tapestry and what they represent. And when she commits suicide we, like Rembrandt, maintain a double vision of what that decision reveals, seeing it at once as a type of heroism that we admire and a type of misguided melodrama that, for all our sympathy, we deplore.

Even more divided are our reactions to Brutus. On one level, we feel grateful when he appears, welcoming this human version of the deux ex machina with a kind of relief that mirrors and helps us to understand the way he is accepted by the "wond'ring" (1845) spectators. One reason our responses are so positive is that his emotional self-control and political shrewdness contrast so strikingly with the helplessness of those around him; in both literal and metaphoric senses, he brings articulateness to the speechless.

What we are experiencing at the end of *The Rape of Lucrece* is, then, the psychological need that corresponds to—and helps to explain—the literary phenomenon of closure: we want tumult to be quieted, pain to be assuaged, and Brutus promises to do all that. In short, we react to him with the pleasure we experience when we encounter the prosodic equivalent to his behavior, the couplet that closes a sonnet or a scene in a play. But if Brutus effects a kind of closure, like the couplet he does so at the price closure so often demands: he conceals the facts that may interfere with the ending he hopes to bring about, reshaping events to conform to the pattern he has predetermined. In this he may remind us of Fortinbras, whose epitaph on Hamlet is as inappropriate on one level as it is reassuring on another. And we may also recall the behavior of Shreve at the end of *Absalom, Absalom!*— or even that of the psychiatrist at the end of *Psycho*. Though their motives are less disturbing than Brutus', these figures are, like him, outsiders who vainly attempt to understand and summarize events very foreign to their sensibilities. Such characters are common enough—and important enough—in literature to merit a category in our anatomy of criticism.

Just as our responses to couplets may be divided, so our judgments on Brutus are very ambivalent; if we seek neat and reassuring conclusions, we also come to distrust them, looking askance at the man who promises to make the trains run on time. Yet the grounds for our distrust remain at best problematical: we need—and do not receive—more information about Brutus' motives in order to reach a balanced judgment. For all its apparent decisiveness, in certain regards the poem ends indeterminately. And so the abruptness of its conclusion both mirrors and intensifies the sense of unease Brutus has produced in us since his initial appearance, much as the ending of *Venus and Adonis* heightens our suspicions about Venus and her mode of effecting closure.

Our ambivalence about Brutus reminds us once more how complex human motivations are—and hence how difficult moral decisions can be. We are, in short, shown yet again that syneciosis is a surer model for the world than Lucrece's forms of antithesis, that predication is likely to be deceptive, and that those who, like Lucrece, attempt to ignore these truths do so at their peril. The poem, then, forces its readers to view, or review, the very truths that its title character is resisting. Another effect of our changing impressions of the principal characters is to lead us to perform a feat that Gestalt psychologists would deem impossible: to see the plot as assuming two different configurations at once. To the extent that we approve of Brutus' actions, the terrible events that preceded them enjoy some sort of resolution at the end of the poem, while to the extent that we distrust him we experience a sense of irresolution again similar to that engendered by Venus' flight at the end of *Venus and Adonis*. This double vision of the contours of *The Rape of Lucrece* parallels a broader pattern in the poem: as we will shortly see, Shakespeare explores historiography and poesy itself by juxtaposing several different modes of writing about Lucrece, each of which is marked by a distinctive approach to closure.

His methods of characterization in his second narrative poem resemble those in *Venus and Adonis* in another way as well: he repeatedly creates what is in effect a dialogic situation by attributing to his characters words with a second meaning of which they are unaware. Through this form of irony he plays two readings against each other—the meaning intended by the personages and the meaning that the reader thinks they should have intended—in much the same way that, as we will see, he plays different versions of the plot itself against each other.

One measure of how much Tarquin deceives himself is that his speech is full of examples of irony. Take, for instance, a passage we have already examined in a different context:

> Quoth he, "She took me kindly by the hand,
> And gaz'd for tidings in my eager eyes,
> Fearing some hard news from the warlike band
> Where her beloved Collatinus lies.
> O how her fear did make her color rise!"
>
> (253–257)

And Tarquin proceeds for nine more lines to anatomize Lucrece's fear. The reader's reaction is that her wifely concern for her husband is—and is being cited as—a telling argument against the rape. Hence we are shocked to discover that Tarquin is in fact employing it in the opposite way; his description of Lucrece is followed immediately by the rhetorical question "Why hunt I then for colour or excuses?" (267). The logical adverb "then" functions ironically, reminding us just how illogical the connection that Tarquin is making really is.

In other instances the ambiguities in Tarquin's language create a different but related interplay of meanings. Vacillating about the rape, he exclaims, "O impious act including all foul harms!" (199). While it is impossible to be sure whether he is thinking about harms to himself, to her, or to both, the fact that the two preceding lines have focused on how the rape would hurt the rapist encourages us to accept the first interpretation. In so doing, however, we become acutely conscious of the potential meaning that he is apparently neglecting—the rape will harm its victim—and of the self-centeredness that the neglect manifests. The possibility that he intends to refer to her remains, of course, but even in that case the fact that he chooses a phrase that could apply to his own conduct reveals the underlying self-centeredness that we observed. Similarly, only two lines later Tarquin declares, "True valour still a true respect should have" (201). "Valour" here may retain certain meanings that are now obsolete, such as "discrimination" or "attention given to more than one point"; but its most obvious denotation, "deferential regard or esteem," is surely also present. When read as an allusion to deference, the line lends itself to two very different glosses, "True valour should always receive true respect" and "True valour should always show true respect to others," and in this case the immediate context does not help us choose one over the other. If we assume Tarquin is interested in others' respect for him rather than in his respect for his victim, we are yet again reminded of how little he cares for Lucrece. If instead we assume he is speaking about her, the presence of an undercurrent of self-centered emotion is as revealing as it was in his statement two lines earlier. And if we assume that he intends both meanings, or consciously chooses to express one while unwittingly expressing the other because it is on his mind, then the tension between the two glosses precisely enacts the tension between the arrogant and self-serving side of the king's son on the one hand and the moral principles with which he is struggling on the other.

Shakespeare also uses such interplays of meaning to evoke contradictory impulses within Lucrece, or, alternatively, the conflicts between her interpretations of experience and those of the reader. Thus the narrator explains why Lucrece does not mention the rape when she writes to Collatine:

> She dares not thereof make discovery,
>   Lest he should hold it her own gross abuse,
>   Ere she with blood had stain'd her stain'd excuse.
>   (1314–1316)

He is using indirect discourse to express the way she views her suicide: her blood will "stain" in the sense of mark the deed that is itself stained in that it involves the letting of blood. But the word "stain" and its cognates have resonated through the whole poem, and when we read those lines we are conscious of a meaning that the word often assumes, both in this poem in particular and in speech in general: to blemish or discolor. According to this interpretation, her suicide is a tragic mistake: her blood is, appropriately enough, a blemish on a deed that is already blemished in the sense of being morally ambiguous. Hence this passage, like many of the others we have examined, embodies a conflict between how we perceive the events of the story and how its participants do.

—Heather Dubrow, *Captive Victors: Shakespeare's Narrative Poems and Sonnets*. (Ithaca, NY: Cornell University Press, 1987), pp. 128–132.

Summary Analysis of
Venus and Adonis

Shakespeare called *Venus and Adonis* "the first heire of my invention" in his dedication to his patron, Henry Wriothesley, third Earl of Southampton. He probably composed the poem during the latter part of 1592, when London's theaters were temporarily closed to prevent the spread of the plague. *Venus and Adonis* was enormously popular: by 1602, 7 editions had been printed, with 16 more published by 1614. The poem then faded into obscurity until critical acclaim brought renewed interest in the 19th century.

Venus and Adonis belongs to a genre of Ovidian mythological-erotic poems. In Ovid's *Metamorphoses*, Book 10 tells how Venus, the goddess of love, woos the handsome young mortal, Adonis. Ovid's brief treatment of the tale presents Venus's seduction of Adonis as successful. Shakespeare's lengthier version, however, chronicles Venus's utter failure to charm Adonis. He resists her because he is too shy and immature for courtship. When he is slain by a wild boar while hunting, his body melts away, leaving a purple and white flower, called anemone, in its place. The goddess plucks it and wears it in her bosom.

Shakespeare wrote *Venus and Adonis* in six-line stanzas, which Thomas Lodge had used in 1589. The rhyme scheme is *ababcc.*

The narrator introduces Venus to us as "sick-thoughted" (5) with love for "Rose-cheeked" (3) Adonis. Hunting is the beautiful youth's passion; "love he laughed to scorn" (4). Venus approaches him and urges him to dismount from his horse and sit by her so that she can "smother [him] with kisses" (18), but he refuses to engage in "such time-beguiling sport" (24). So the goddess snatches Adonis from his horse, tucks him under one arm, pins him to the ground and holds him there, "And govern'd him in strength, though not in lust" (42). Adonis, for his part, lies in her arms like "a bird lies tangled in a net" (67).

She forces unreciprocated kisses upon him. When she realizes that force alone will not work, Venus tries several oratorical strategies. First, she boasts that the god of war himself was the willing captive of her charms (97–114). When that fails, she exhorts Adonis not to waste his own beauty: "Fair flowers that are not gathered in their prime/ Rot, and consume themselves in little time" (131–132). Then she wonders at his lack of ardor for her own considerable beauty: "But having no defects, why dost abhor me?" she asks (138). Finally, Venus urges him to do his "duty" and beget offspring with her (163–174). But Adonis interjects with, "Fie, no more of love!/ The sun doth burn my face, I must remove"(185–6). But Venus continues to woo him, her language full of erotic metaphors in an effort to awaken Adonis's desire. Unmoved, Adonis jumps up and runs for his horse.

But at that moment, his stallion, having seen and heard a jennet [small Spanish horse] nearby, breaks his leather tong and gallops to her. This digression strengthens the narrative because the jennet's coyness and the stallion's mad pursuit of her are juxtaposed with Venus's doomed advances to an unresponsive Adonis.

Without his horse, Adonis is trapped as Venus continues her pleas of love. But Adonis shoots her such a scornful look that she faints. Having only meant to rebuke her, he fearfully kneels beside her to revive her—with comical results:

> He wrings her nose, he strikes her on the cheeks,
> He bends her fingers, holds her pulses hard;
> He chafes her lips; a thousand ways he seeks
> To mend the hurt that his unkindness marred.
> > He kisses her; and she, by her good will,
> > Will never rise, so he will kiss her still.
>
> (475–480)

Upon recovering from her swoon, the goddess simply begs for the youth's affections. "To sell myself I would be well contented," she tells him (513). Adonis makes a moving plea to the goddess to take his youth and inexperience into account:

> "Fair Queen," quoth he, "if any love you owe me,
> Measure my strangeness with my unripe years;
> Before I know myself, seek not to know me:
> No fisher but the ungrown fry forbears;
> > The mellow plum doth fall, the green sticks fast,
> > Or being early pluck'd, is sour to taste.
>
> (523–528)

Venus reluctantly agrees to part with him for the night. For this, Adonis rewards her with a kiss. She kisses him so passionately that they fall to the ground as one. When he finally extricates himself from her, Venus asks when they can meet the next day. Adonis replies that he is going boar hunting. But she throws her arms around his neck, so "he on her belly falls, she on her back" (594). The narrator observes that "She's love, she loves, yet she is not lov'd" (610). Adonis cannot bear any more of Venus's "love": "Fie, fie, you crush me. Let me go. / You have no reason to hold me so" (611–612).

Although a goddess, Venus is remarkably powerless here. She cannot even seduce. Still, she can prophesy:

> I prophesy thy death, my living sorrow,
> If thou encounter with the boar tomorrow.
>
> (671–672)

Yet the goddess is helpless in the face of her prophecy. Venus launches into a fearsome description of the boar, and of the terrors faced by Wat the hare when he becomes the hunter's prey. Although she warns Adonis of his impending death—and tries to frighten him into heeding her—he runs off into the darkness to hunt, anyway.

The next morning finds Venus in the woods frantically searching for the youth. In the distance she hears the frightened cries of the dogs: she sees the boar, his "frothy mouth bepainted all with red" (901). The goddess first denounces death as a "Hard-favour'd tyrant, ugly, meagre, lean,/Hateful divorce of love" (931–932). But she backpedals upon hearing the distant cry of a hunter, vainly hoping that it is Adonis:

"No, no," quoth she, "sweet death, I did but jest;
Yet pardon me, I felt a kind of fear
Whenas I met the boar, that bloody beast,
Which knows no pity, but is still severe."
                                        (997–1000)

Shakespeare uses an extended simile that likens Venus to a snail as she reacts to the sight of the slain Adonis:

Or as the snail, whose tender horns being hit,
Shrinks backward in his shelly cave with pain,
And there all smother'd up in shade doth sit,
Long after fearing to creep forth again.
        So at his bloody view her eyes are fled
        Into the deep dark cabins of her head.
                                        (1033–1038)

The goddess—who has not yet been at a loss for words—is initially unable to express her grief. She then manages to deliver a sincere elegy for Adonis, followed by a spiteful prophecy. Through Venus's prophecy, the narrator explains how love became so turbulent and heartbreaking for humankind:

It shall suspect where is no cause of fear;
It shall not fear where it should most mistrust.
It shall be merciful, and too severe,
And most deceiving when it seems most just.
        Perverse it shall be, where it shows most toward,
        Put fear to valour, courage to the coward.

It shall be cause of war and dire events,
And set dissension twixt the son and sire;
Subject and servile to all discontents,
As dry combustious matter is to fire.
        Sith in his prime death doth my love destroy,
        They that love best, their loves shall not enjoy.
                                        (1153–1164)

This said, Adonis's body "Was melted like a vapour from her sight" (1166). In his blood, a purple flower springs up. The goddess bows to smell it, compares it to Adonis's breath, then breaks the flower off by the stalk and takes it to her bosom:

My throbbing heart shall rock thee day and night
        There shall not be one minute in an hour
        Wherein I will not kiss my sweet love's flower.
                                        (1186–1188)

The weary queen of love then boards her chariot vanishes into the sky.

In *Venus and Adonis*, Shakespeare creates a sense of playfulness between the two would-be lovers that will color his later work. As critics since Coleridge have noted, the Bard's detachment from his characters and from the story is obvious. Even in this early work, we "seem to be told nothing, but to see everything." ❁

Critical Views on
Venus and Adonis

JONATHAN BATE ON SHAKESPEARE'S RHETORIC OF
DESIRE

[Jonathan Bate is King Alfred Professor of English Literature at the
University of Liverpool. His books include *Shakespeare and the English Romantic Imagination* (1989) and *Shakespeare and Ovid* (1993),
from which this extract is taken.]

Venus doesn't metamorphose herself into the boar in the manner of Jupiter
becoming an animal in order to rape a mortal girl. The story is about frus-
tration rather than violation because a woman can't rape a man. The tone is
set not by the spilling of blood towards the end, but by the earlier sequences
in which the violence is playful and nobody really gets hurt: 'Backward she
pushed him, as she would be thrust" (41). For much of *Venus and Adonis*,
sexual desire is a source of comedy, whereas Shakespeare's second narrative
poem is unquestionably tragic because Tarquin does rape Lucrece. The
story of sexual pursuit is replayed in a darker key; having made a comic
spectacle of the rapacious goddess, Shakespeare makes a tragic spectacle of
the raped emblem of chastity. The two poems are opposite sides of the same
coin, as may be seen from their structural resemblance: in each, an ardent
suitor attempts to gain the reluctant object of his/her sexual desire by
means of rhetorical persuasion, fails, and indirectly or directly precipitates
the death of the object of desire. The difference between the two is that
Adonis dies with his chastity intact—he is only metaphorically raped by the
boar—while Lucrece stabs herself because she has been ravished. But both
poems are centrally interested in the way in which, as in Ovid's *Amores* and
Ars Amatoria, linguistic art is instrumental in the pursuit of sexual satisfac-
tion. *The Rape of Lucrece* is not only Shakespeare's most sustained imitation,
it is also a supreme example of Renaissance *copia*. . . .

As in *Venus and Adonis*, Shakespeare's principal interest is the psychology
of desire. The moment in Ovid from which he begins is that when Tarquin
catches sexual fire. A longish quotation. . . is needed here in order to show
how Shakespeare built on not merely a narrative and a psychology, but also
a rhetoric:

> Meantime the royal youth caught fire and fury, and transported by
> blind love he raved. Her figure pleased him, and that snowy hue, that
> yellow hair, and artless grace; pleasing, too, her words and voice and
> virtue incorruptible; and the less hope he had, the hotter his desire.
> Now had the bird, the herald of the dawn, uttered his chant, when the
> young men retraced their steps to camp. Meantime the image of his
> absent love preyed on his senses crazed. In memory's light more fair
> and fair she grew. ' 'Twas thus she sat, 'twas thus she dressed, 'twas
> thus she spun the threads, 'twas thus her tresses careless lay upon her
> neck; that was her look, these were her words, that was her colour,
> that her form, and that her lovely face.' After a great gale the surge

subsides, and yet the billow heaves, lashed by the wind now fallen, so, though absent now that winsome form and far away, the love which by its presence it had struck into his heart remained. He burned, and, goaded by the pricks of an unrighteous love, he plotted violence and guile against an innocent bed. 'The issue is in doubt. We'll dare the utmost,' said he. 'Let her look to it! God and fortune help the daring. By daring we captured Gabii too.'

This passage is like Shakespeare's poem—or rather the first half of Shakespeare's poem—in miniature. It is driven by ardour. As 'ignis' ('fire') and 'ardet' ('he burned') are key words here, so Shakespeare from his first stanza onward plays persistently on Tarquin's heat:

> From the besieged Ardea all in post,
> Born by the trustless wings of false desire,
> Lust-breathèd Tarquin leaves the Roman host
> And to Collatium bears the lightless fire
> Which, in pale embers hid, lurks to aspire
> And girdle with embracing flames the waist
> Of Collatine's fair love, Lucrece the chaste.
>
> (1–7)

The first line seems to introduce a pun that Ovid could well have made but didn't; the city which the Romans happen to be besieging is *Ard*ea and its name prepares the reader for Tarquin's seuxal *ard*our.

—Jonathan Bate, *Shakespeare and Ovid.* (Oxford: Clarendon Press, 1993), pp. 65–69.

RICHARD LANHAM ON THE NARRATOR'S DETACHMENT

[Richard Lanham, Professor of English at the University of California in Los Angeles, is the author of *Sidney's Old Arcadia, Handlist of Rhetorical Terms, Tristram Shandy: The Games of Pleasure, Revising Prose,* and *Analyzing Prose.* He is also the author of *The Motives of Eloquence: Literary Rhetoric in the Renaissance* (1976), from which this extract is taken.]

Dramatic characterization, then, is only part of the story. Both Venus and Adonis have a mythic character too, and a rhetoric queasily in between. The whole character of each encloses a paradoxical, inconsistent, comic combination of all three. Shakespeare has imitated man acting, man talking, man talking about acting, man's acting being largely talk ("Your treatise makes me like you worse and worse" [l. 774]). The rhetoric of the poem has been dramatized, made part of the story, Venus a Venus Genetrix of words. Adonis is not only short on deeds, but on words. When Venus explodes with surprise at a sudden burst of speech from the hero, we share her feelings: "'What! canst thou talk?' quoth she. 'Hast thou a tongue?'" (l. 427). So much

of the poem's action is talk that the two blend in our minds, we confuse res-
olute action with volubility. To talk well is to be alive, to see, hear, feel. To all
of these, serious, inarticulate Adonis is insensitive. Venus really creates with
her own praise the Adonis who can represent beauty. She creates herself
with her own praise. She creates the significance of Adonis's death by her
descriptive sorrow. She creates everything. Her eloquence dominates the
poem. Only she can give meaning, not only to her desire for Adonis, but to
his for the boar. Her poetic powers in the poem stand as synecdoche for her
fructifying powers in the world.

Coleridge, in chapter fifteen of the *Biographia*, emphasizes Shakespeare's
detachment from his poem, "the utter aloofness of the poet's own feelings."
But Shakespeare's voice in the poem, the narrator, portrays not so much
aloofness as neutrality, a position amidships the bathos and the pathos, a
careful trimming. Look at the first stanza in the poem:

> Even as the sun with purple-colored face
> Had ta'en his last leave of the weeping morn,
> Rose-cheeked Adonis hied him to the chase.
> Hunting he loved, but love he laughed to scorn.
>> Sick-thoughted Venus makes amain to him
>> And like a bold-faced suitor 'gins to woo him.

The first two lines belong to the neutral ground of the poem's action; the
next two (especially in the simpering chiasmus of line four) to the adolescent Adonis; the last two, to the cosmic Venus. The narrator gives everyone
his due, keeps his distance, lets the reader sort the indecorums out. The
smooth stylistic surface forms part of this distancing strategy. It is brilliant.
It reflects. We see in it the premises we bring to it.

The narrator makes of his own cleverness a defense. He does not, as mask
for Shakespeare, speak straighforwardly any more than Venus and Adonis.
To preoccupy ourselves with "Shakespeare's" feelings, to apply the litmus
paper of sincerity, we must examine the whole poem, the interaction of the
three rhetorics comprising it. Adonis has his point of view. Venus has hers,
which contradicts it. We may think hers the more comprehensive, or his.
What does the narrator think of Venus and Adonis? The careful centrality of
his diction makes it impossible to tell.

> Forced to content, but never to obey
> Panting he lies and breatheth in her face.
> She feedeth on the steam as on a prey
> And calls it heavenly moisture, air of grace,
>> Wishing her cheeks were gardens full of flowers,
>> So they were dewed with such distilling showers.
>>> [ll. 61–66]

The narrator calls the scene as he sees it. Adonis pants and breathes in
Venus's face and she makes of it heavenly moisture, air of grace. He shows
no signs of noticing that after the second line we notice a change in tone.
He is deaf to tone though he faithfully reports it; he can mirror but he

cannot comprehend. What does the narrator think of Venus and Adonis? He does not think at all.

What do we think of him? He possesses a rich poetic power but no judgment to go with it. To him Shakespeare has lent his pen but not his mind. Such a divorce, perfect though it is for a satire of love and love's language, has caused serious misunderstanding. The narrator's view has been thought Shakespeare's. *Venus and Adonis* is a complex rhetorical structure to which sincerity supplies the wrong entry. The complaints about insincerity show the need to discriminate the three rhetorics of the poem, describe what each does, and specify their relationship. The narrator is Ovidian indeed. He springs surprises on us in the couplet. He condenses within the line by chiasmus, ploce, polyptoton. He models sense in syntax. He describes both Venus and Adonis with the tone appropriate to each. Thus a constantly shifting decorum is preserved. Shakespeare sees all three characters and beyond, arranges the comic juxtapositions, remains—like Ovid—completely in control. Far from being infatuated with rhetoric, he fashions a mature satire in which it becomes a principal target.

The poem's comedy tempts us to deny it any seriousness whatever, to blunt its pathos, render it a perfect trifle, Shakespeare's comedy of language. But the comedy does not explain or explain away the pathos of Adonis's death. If Shakespeare had in mind straightforward romantic comedy, why choose such a story as that of Venus and Adonis? And, having chosen it, why expatiate upon the "trembling ecstasy" Venus undergoes before and during the boar hunt? Why, instead of romantic comedy's redemption of love, offer his story as exemplum for future horrors of love? Still more, why couch those horrors in cosmic terms? "For he being dead, with him is beauty slain, / And, beauty dead, black chaos comes again" (ll. 1019–20). If tone guides us to the poem, tone here has changed. Why include such pathos only to cancel it?

> —Richard Lanham, *The Motives of Eloquence: Literary Rhetoric in the Renaissance.* (New Haven, CT: Yale University Press, 1976), pp. 88–91.

⊕

NANCY LINDHEIM ON VULNERABILITY AND POWERLESS NESS IN THE POEM

[In this essay, Nancy Lindheim examines the ways that Shakespeare changed the character of Ovid's Adonis to heighten the distinctions between him and Venus, and to make the power imbalance between them sharper.]

Shakespeare seems to have decided that the way to examine metamorphosis in a comic mode is to reinterpret the implications of the word. The metamorphic paradigm is no longer nymph into laurel tree or white into purple berry, but tadpole into frog or caterpillar into butterfly. This too is an indication of new directions in Shakespeare's thought, for the idea is intrinsic to the comedies that follow: we may well be reminded of the three young men of Navarre who believe themselves to be at a stage where the totally male pursuits of Platonic study are still feasible, but even closer are the connections with another work pervaded by Ovid's *Metamorphoses, A Midsummer Night's Dream*. C. L. Barber has beautifully demonstrated the way in which the idea of maturation is central to that play: e.g., in the exchange of girlhood ties (growing like two cherries on a stem) for marriage, or in the propriety of the young Indian page's giving up the maternal protection of Titania's band to become a knight in Oberon's train.

Reconceiving Ovid's Adonis (who is explicitly not *puer* but *iuvenis*, i.e., a young man in his twenties) so that he is an adolescent may well have been the crucial fact in Shakespeare's transformation of the story. It heightens both the comedy and the pathos of Adonis, depending on whether one views him in relation to Venus or to the boar. With Venus, as we have seen, the disparity between her vigorous sensuality and his standoffish refusal to place himself psychologically at risk gives rise to a spectrum of comedy that runs from tenderness to titillation and frank vulgarity. In terms of the boar, however, this sheltered innocence emphasizes Adonis's vulnerability both to time (the boar is traditionally a figure of winter) and to death. Perhaps paradoxically, his status as Beauty is focused more sharply, certainly more poignantly, when he is pursued by Time than by Love.

Compared to Ovid's, Shakespeare's version seems more firmly rooted in the double tradition of Adonis as ritual figure of vegetative myth and as poetic subject of elegy. Both traditions (the second of course growing from the first) hinge on Adonis's mortality. The pathos of the elegiac tradition depends on the perfection of the creature who has died through no fault of his own and in defiance of what is called "justice" in the universe. Underlying the myth is a fertility ritual that tries to influence the process of vegetative death and rebirth, of seasonal fallowness and harvest, with sexual links clear enough to become the basis of Spenser's Garden of Adonis. The relations among the elements in the triad of innocence-sexuality-death are not simple or punitive: the elegiac tradition reminds us that Adonis's tragedy inheres not in the loss of innocence but of life. It is possible for Adonis to feel that the boar and Venus are equally his enemies, and it is possible for Venus to see in the boar's nuzzling of Adonis with his tusk an analogue to her own sexual desires, but the reader has learned to see these reductive views as part of a larger complexity. Adonis the dying god is scapegoat, not criminal, and Adonis the dying shepherd-hunter is also innocent of harm; both are victims of "Nature," as is Shakespeare's adolescent. Though it is abstractly possible to see the boar's association with the violence of both sexuality and time (its identification with lust and death) as causally related, it seems to me to destroy the narrative integrity of the poem to do so. Both the logic of the story itself and the most pressing meanings arising from it encourage one to understand the boar as something outside Adonis and not projected from his psyche. "Devouring Time," which "feeds on the rarities of nature's truth," is the force that interests Shakespeare, in 1593 as well as later. Neither the original tradition nor the poem as written provides support for a punitive reading of the story. Adonis is not killed for what he does but for what he is. In Yeats's words, "Man is in love and loves what he wishes, / What more is there to say?"

That Adonis is locked into nature I take to be of primary importance to the poem; in addition to allowing Shakespeare to escape a narrow punitive moralism, it affords him the setting, metaphors, and digressions for realizing a relation between lover and beloved that will be worked out more intensively in the middle sonnets. Although the obvious parallels between *Venus and Adonis* and the *Sonnets* are with the early "procreative" group, the sonnets on mutability and those exploring the psychological dependence and virtual helplessness of the lover can also be seen as a mature development of the implications of *Venus and Adonis*. In the conception of both Adonis and the Young Man of the *Sonnets*, two things are critical: (1) their beauty, which becomes a sign or symbol for whatever the lover finds valuable and sustaining in the world (clearer in the Sonnets, but surely the meaning of Venus's assertion that after Adonis's death "black Chaos comes again") and (2) their mortality. As in Keats, this is "Beauty that must die."

The realization of mutability—its full terror and how man must live in the shadow of its inevitable loss—is merely adumbrated in this poem. More fully developed is the *Sonnets'* constant recourse to nature for pattern and interpretation of experience, as well as for analogies to the value that the poet perceives. Beauty, however moral and spiritual we would make it by extension, is first a material quality for Shakespeare, existing in nature before man creates it in art. His paradigms for the experiences of human love would lie in nature even if Adonis were not by origin a figure from vegetative myth. They are to be seen in the round of the sun, the course of the seasons, the life of a flower, the joyful lark, the stallion's sexual instinct, the isolation and fear of a hunted hare, the destructiveness of a wild boar, the rapacious eagle, the need of a milch doe to feed her fawn, the snail "Shrink[ing] backward in his shelly cave with pain" (l. 1034).

Two long digressions—the episode of the horses and Venus's lecture on Wat the hare—inconceivable in a poem like *Hero and Leander* or *Glaucus and Scilla*, are thus fully constant with Shakespeare's conception of *Venus and Adonis*. Thematically the function of the horses is easier to understand than that of the hare, in which we are perhaps to feel our powerlessness against the forces that bring death. Adonis, like Wat, will soon be a victim of the hunt; even Venus herself, the goddess tied to a mortal, becomes associated with Wat's plight as she rushes through the forest to confirm her fearful premonition. She too is caught and scratched by bushes in her way (ll. 871–71), she too "treads the path that she untreads again" (l. 908). Adonis's stallion defiantly asserts control of his actions when he breaks his rein at the urging of sexual instinct, but he is no more master than is the hunted hare. All are within nature's dominion, even Venus insofar as her "life" depends on the mortal Adonis.

—Nancy Lindheim, "The Shakespearean *Venus and Adonis*." In *Shakespeare Quarterly* 37 (1986): pp. 196–198.

HEATHER DUBROW ON HOW THE POET SHAPES OUR RESPONSES

[Heather Dubrow, Professor of English at Carleton College in Northfield, Minnesota, is the author of *Genre* (1982). She is also the author of *Captive Victors: Shakespeare's Narrative Poems and Sonnets* (1987), from which this extract is taken. Dubrow examines the connections between the sonnets and the narrative poems, pointing out that Shakespeare uses rhetoric to create characters as rich in complexities as those found in his dramatic works.]

We have repeatedly touched on one of the sharpest and yet most subtle distinctions between *Venus and Adonis* and other epyllia: the audience's reactions to their respective characters. Recent students of reader response criticism have offered salutary warnings about the difficulties of mapping those reactions; we are not, so to speak, all surprised by sin at the same time or in the same way or to the same extent. In this instance, it is certainly true that the sex of the reader—or, indeed, his or her attitudes to sex—may influence the relevant responses to Shakespeare's characters. But such factors are more likely merely to affect the intensity of our responses to Venus and Adonis than to determine their nature, for, as we will see, on the whole the language of the poem effectively guides our reactions to its protagonists. And its success in doing so emerges clearly if we once again play Shakespeare's Ovidian narrative against those written by his contemporaries.

Despite all the other shifts in tone and attitude that characterize the work of these writers, they only rarely invite us to experience real sympathy for their characters. The poems most closely modeled on complaints, *Scillaes Metamorphosis* and *Oenone and Paris,* are, predictably enough, exceptions, but in a sense they are exceptions that prove the rule: here the appeals for sympathy are so frequently and so clumsily extended that for this reason alone we do not feel very much of it. In any event, in most epyllia we are distanced from the situations by blatant reminders of their fictionality. Above all, however, we sympathize only rarely with the characters in these poems because we are invited instead into a kind of complicity with the superior, even supercilious, narrators. At times this complicity is anchored in a knowing distrust of women. Marlowe establishes the trend, and many of his followers participate in it:

> Still vowed he love, she wanting no excuse
> To feed him with delaies, as women use:
> Or thirsting after immortalitie,
> All women are ambitious naturallie:
>> (Marlowe, *Hero and Leander* l. 425–428)

>> Tut, women will relent
> When they finde such mouing blandishment.
> (Marston, *The Metamorphosis of Pigmalions Image,* 173–174)

> In womens mouths, No is no negative.
>> (Weever, *Faunus and Melliflora,* sig. C2)

Nor do the male characters escape the ironic appraisal of the narrator, and in this too the reader participates: the speaker's wry judgments on them, like some of the asides Richard III addresses to the audience, encourage us to contrast our own knowingness with the inexperience of the blinded characters before us. One thinks above all of the dramatic irony established by Leander's sexual innocence—"he suspected / Some amorous rites or other were neglected" (ll. 63–64) or, similarly, of Dunstan Gale's "But let her lye alone, / For other pastime *Pyramus* knew none" (*Pyramus and Thisbe*, 51–52).

If these poems do not invite sympathy toward their characters, neither do they encourage reflection on most of the issues those personages might raise. . . .

When we read *Venus and Adonis,* in contrast, our responses to the characters seesaw as rapidly as the tenses do. As my analyses have suggested, within a stanza, or even within a line, we may move back and forth between sympathetic identification and intense repulsion. Yet we never read on for long without feeling a surge of sympathy: for much of the poem it is a kind of basso continuo against which our other reactions are played. Given how readily both characters would lend themselves to cold caricature—Adonis's sexual innocence, for example, would be a ready target for the knowing narrators in other epyllia—creating and maintaining this sympathy are among the principal achievements of the poem. No less of an achievement, however, is its ability to elicit from us trenchant ethical judgments on the very characters with whom we are sympathizing.

> —Heather Dubrow, *Captive Victors: Shakespeare's Narrative Poems and Sonnets.* (Ithaca, NY: Cornell University Press, 1987), pp. 62–65.

⊛

JOHN KLAUSE ON WHY VENUS AND ADONIS CAN BE REDEEMED

[In this essay, John Klause argues that despite the influences of an unrelenting fate and the serious flaws in their characters, Venus and Adonis are not past the point of redemption, and that they have the potential to break out of the roles set for them.]

In *Venus and Adonis* a very strong impression is conveyed that its characters are diminutive and helpless before the large forces that finally defeat them. The poem offers reasons enough to believe that the "Destinies" have worked "To cross the curious workmanship of Nature" (734). Like Marvell's parallels that never meet, Venus and Adonis in acting out what they are seem doomed to the most flagrant incompatibility. And for a goddess, Venus is remarkably uninformed and powerless. She can "prohpesy" (671, 1135) but is helpless in the face of prophecy. Her ignorance of Adonis' whereabouts and condition allows her to be toyed with by "Death," whom she first vainly excoriates then humbly tries to appease. When Adonis disappears, dissolving into the night—

> Look how a bright star shooteth from the sky,
> So glides he in the night from Venus' eye,

> Which after him she darts, as one on shore
> Gazing after a late embarked friend,
> Till the wild waves will have him seen no more,
> Whose ridges with the meeting clouds contend;
> So did the merciless and pitchy night
> Fold in the object that did feed her sight—
>
> (815–22)

we are given an acute sense of how massively formidable the darkness can be, and how puny are those who try to resist it.

The lowly may be pitied; ultimately, however, the most persuasive invitation in this stanza to proceed beyond sympathy to forgiveness lies not in the fact that the "night" is overwhelmingly large, but that it is characteristically "merciless" (821). Will the good, in order to be itself, have to match in ruthlessness its adversary? Although pardon is moved by nothing so much as by the generosity of the one who grants it, the refusal to forgive does not necessarily place one among the forces of unloving darkness. Yet by showing these powers to be without mercy, Shakespeare at least suggests that the opportunity to oppose them through an act of charity is a salutary temptation. Yielding to it may not be for a reader a terribly formal or conscious act, but it would be in light of the poem's whole truth a crucial one.

Forgiveness of Venus and Adonis must in a way be more radical than usual, because the characters do not conveniently confess and repent. Adonis remains shallow and obstinate to the end. Venus never questions the legitimacy of her passions, never regrets her onslaughts, and never quite attains a self-abnegating respect for the rights and privileges of another. Indeed, in her sour leavetaking after Adonis' death, she may seem extravagantly mean-spirited, hardly of a disposition to inspire in an accommodating observer a sympathetic attitude:

> Sith in his prime death doth my life destroy,
> They that love best their loves shall not enjoy.
>
> (1163–64)

A scrupulous reading of the poem, however, and a consideration of the ideal of forgiveness in itself suggest that these "obstacles" to pardon are not insuperable. In the first place, when Venus catalogues the woes that love will suffer in the wake of her disappointment, she is not uttering a curse but a prophecy ("Since thou art dead, lo here I prophesy. . ." [1135]). She does not in her grief blindly revenge herself on subsequent generations of lovers (she has in fact been shown to be quite powerless), any more than she contributes to Adonis' death by predicting it (671). Love shall be attended by "sorrow," shall "Bud, and be blasted, in a breathing while," shall "be sparing, and too full of riot," shall cause "dissension" and a host of other ills (1135-64)—not because Venus will maliciously produce them but because an archetypal and imperfect Love has already suffered them, or something like them. We should not hold her bitterness against her. In the second place, even if from the moral point of view Venus and Adonis are not wholly admirable, they are not by that fact excluded from the beneficience of mercy. As Augustine pointed out (believing with St. Paul in a God who forgives sinners not because they have become virtuous but because they are redeemable: "Christ died for the ungodly. . . . While we were yet sinners, Christ died for us" [Rom. 5:8]), pardon does not have to wait for reform. As long as wickedness is not in characters an absolutely final state, forgiveness does not irresponsibly or perversely sanction "the evil that men do.". . .

Venus and Adonis does not seem to present . . . a "justification" of mercy, for if in the poem there are inducements enough to such conviction and faith, there are no obvious grounds for such hope. Adonis, after all, dies with no new knowledge and essentially unchanged. Venus retreats into what appears to be a permanent malaise, certain, as her prophecy indicates, to remain what she is. Are not the follies and iniquities of these characters "final"? Not if Venus and Adonis can be seen as part of ourselves and our world—not, that is, if the poet has succeeded in creating characters who are at once sufficiently distant from us to allow criticism and sufficiently close (as mythical embodiments of possibilities in human character or in the world of values) to warrant the acknowledgment that their imperfections and dilemmas are our own. Venus and Adonis, then, would be "hopeless" cases only were we so; and as long as we are not, *they* may be forgiven, even as we may have mercy on ourselves.

> —John Klause, "Venus and Adonis: Can We Forgive Them?" In *Studies in Philology* 85 (1988): pp. 373–375.

TITA FRENCH BAUMLIN ON SHAKESPEARE AND HIS PREDECESSORS

[In this essay, Tita French Baumlin discusses the contrast between Shakespeare's Venus and Ovid's, showing how the inept character of Shakespeare's Venus makes her a comic figure, where Ovid's was a commanding one.]

And thus, with kisses to punctuate the tale, [Ovid's] Venus tells the Tale of Atalanta who refused love until the race with Hippomenes, where she learned her own limitations and let love transform her. In Ovid's version, then, the goddess Venus is above all a poet, for it is with her poetry, the tale of Atalanta, that she affects the seduction. Her poetry, however, is naive; it takes for granted precisely what it has to prove: its persuasive power. Ovid is, in fact, himself naive regarding the persuasive power of poetic language: for Ovid, such powers are automatic.

For Shakespeare's self-critical age, however, it is the very power of language which must be proven. Thus the essential difference between Shakespeare's and Ovid's text: the Renaissance poet cannot take such powers for granted but must find and fashion them in the act of composing. As poets find inspiration in their predecessors and yet struggle against them—what Harold Bloom has called the "anxiety of influence"—so does their poetry engage in combat with their sources, as Bloom points out: "The poet's conception of himself necessarily is his poem's conception of itself, in my reading, and central to this conception is the matter of the sources of the powers of poetry," for "the truest sources, again necessarily, are in the powers of poems *already written*." This view of the nature of the poetic art is particularly applicable to the Renaissance poet, who deliberately adopts a pre-existing text as inspiration but must also somehow fashion his own poetic voice in the process. Ben Jonson illustrates such "anxiety of influence" in the age of the English Renaissance:

> A requisite in our *Poet,* or Maker is *imitation,* to be able to convert the substance or Riches of another Poet to his own use. To make choise of one excellent man above the rest, and so to follow him till he grow very *Hee,* or so like him as the Copie may be mistaken for the Principall. Not, as a Creature that swallowes what it takes in, crude, raw, or undigested, but that feedes with an Appetite, and hath a Stomacke to concoct, divide, and turne all to nourishment.

This metaphor—feeding upon the model text in order to turn its material through digestion literally into the body of another text—implies the violence and subversion which J. Hillis Miller finds essential to the composing process, wherein the "host" poem becomes "food, host in the sense of victim, sacrifice":

> The previous text is both the ground of the new one and something the new poem must annihilate by incorporating it, turning it into ghostly insubstantiality, so that the new poem may perform its possible-impossible task of becoming its own ground. The new poem both needs the old texts and must destroy them. It is both parasitical on them, feeding ungraciously on their substance, and at the same time it is the sinister host which unmans them by inviting them into its home.

Thus, markedly different in Shakespeare's account of the wooing is Venus's total lack of success in winning Adonis for her paramour; the emphasis falls, instead, upon the poet's self-conscious attention to her language as she attempts, and fails, to seduce Adonis. Hallett Smith has noted—and lamented—the combative, argumentative nature of Venus's rhetoric, which is "unadapted to the genre" of Ovidian love poetry, for the reader is burdened with Venus's extended discourses—like the one beginning at line 95, where "for eighty lines she discusses Mars, her own charms, Narcissus, torches, jewels, herbs, and the laws of nature which require propagation . . . so that instead of realizing evoked physical beauty we are listening to a lecture." Venus's discourses are indeed the lectures of a pedant, deliberately, if the rhetoric is to reveal important facets of Venus's initially flawed, ineffective character. Of course, this Venus fails to seduce a reader like Hallett Smith, fails to evoke the image of beauty that would entice him to judge her worthy of the same name as the Ovidian Goddess of Love, that would lead him to judge the poem itself as a "successful" Ovidian love poem. Similarly, this Venus fails to seduce a reader like Gordon Williams, who finds that her character is too grotesque in this early portion of the poem to be taken seriously at all. Venus's failure to persuade and seduce modern readers thus mirrors her own failure to seduce Adonis—and ultimately, this failure leads us to question the nature and source of poetic inspiration: from what source—either for Venus or for the poet himself—comes the rhetorical power to seduce? Is it the model that creates, legitimizes, or confirms the new poet? Clearly, the poet's experience of human struggle *against* language as well as with language—the poet's experience of human failure with language—sets in motion the motivations which will occupy the true poet for a lifetime.

> —Tita French Baumlin, "The Birth of the Bard: *Venus and Adonis* and Poetic Apotheosis." In *Papers on Language and Literature* 26 (1990): pp. 193–195.

✦

Jonathan Bate on Ovid's Influence on Shakespeare

[Jonathan Bate is King Alfred Professor of English Literature at the University of Liverpool. His books include *Shakespeare and the English Romantic Imagination* (1989) and *Shakespeare and Ovid* (1993), from which this extract is taken.]

Ovid tells the story of Venus and Adonis in less than a hundred lines, Shakespeare in more than a thousand: the classical text provides a narrative framework into which the Elizabethan writer inserts elaborate arguments, thus demonstrating his own rhetorical skills. Because the persuasions given to the characters are the major interpolations into the source, critical readings tend to concentrate on them. But it will be the contention of the first half of this chapter that within Shakespeare's poem there are signals that we must consider the Ovidian source-text to be much broader than the seventy or so lines of direct material. Golding's outward/inward distinction works differently in Shakespeare's reading of Ovid: whilst the moral translator claimed to find meaning 'inwardlye' but in fact imposed it from outside the text, the creative imitator interprets his source narrative partly by means of other narratives that lie both outside and inside, around and within it. Surrounding the text is a distinctly unwholesome context.

When Shakespeare read Book Ten of the *Metamorphoses*, the first thing he was told about Adonis was that he was the 'misbegotten chyld' of the union between Myrrha and her father, Cinyras. At the same time, he would have learnt that the lovely boy was born not from his mother's womb, but by the splitting open through Lucina's agency of the tree into which his mother had been metamorphosed. Incest and a kind of posthumous cesarean section—a bizarre birth like that of Marvell's 'Unfortunate Lover'—initiate the reader into a world of unorthodox swervings of gender and generation.

> —Jonathan Bate, *Shakespeare and Ovid*. (Oxford: Clarendon Press, 1993), pp. 50–51. ✦

Works by
William Shakespeare

It is almost impossible to date a given play precisely. The following is the list of first performances:

1589–92	*Henry VI Part 1, Henry VI Part 2, Henry VI Part 3*
1592–93	*Richard III, The Comedy of Errors*
1593–94	*Titus Andronicus, The Taming of the Shrew*
1594–95	*The Two Gentlemen of Verona, Love's Labour's Lost, Romeo and Juliet*
1595–96	*Richard II, A Midsummer Night's Dream*
1596–97	*King John, The Merchant of Venice*
1597–98	*Henry IV Part 1, Henry IV Part 2*
1598–99	*Much Ado About Nothing, Henry V*
1599–1600	*Julius Caesar, As You Like It*
1600–01	*Hamlet, The Merry Wives of Windsor*
1601–02	*Twelfth Night, Troilus and Cressida*
1602–03	*All's Well That Ends Well*
1604–05	*Measure for Measure, Othello*
1605–06	*King Lear, Macbeth*
1606–07	*Antony and Cleopatra*
1607–08	*Coriolanus, Timon of Athens*
1608–09	*Pericles*
1609–10	*Cymbeline*
1610–11	*The Winter's Tale*
1611–12	*The Tempest*
1612–13	*Henry VIII, The Two Noble Kinsmen*

Venus and Adonis and *The Rape of Lucrece*, Shakespeare's two narrative poems, can be dated with certainty (1592 and 1593–94, respectively). "The Phoenix and Turtle" can be dated 1600–01. As for the Sonnets, most scholars agree that they were probably written within the period 1593–1600.

The following list indicates a given play's first publication date:

1594	*Henry VI Part 2, Titus Andronicus*
1595	*Henry VI Part 3*
1597	*Richard III, Romeo and Juliet, Richard II*
1598	*Love's Labour's Lost, Henry IV Part 1*
1600	*A Midsummer Night's Dream, The Merchant of Venice, Henry IV Part 2*

	Much Ado About Nothing
	Henry V
1602	*The Merry Wives of Windsor*
1603	*Hamlet*
1608	*King Lear*
1609	*Troilus and Cressida*
	Pericles
1622	*Othello*

Since the texts of *Venus and Adonis* (1593) and *The Rape of Lucrece* (1594) are free of errors, Shakespeare must have furnished a good copy of each to the printer. The collected Sonnets were published in 1609, but we have no evidence that Shakespeare oversaw their publication.

Works about
Shakespeare's Sonnets and Poems

Baldwin, T. W. *On the Literary Genetics of Shakespeare's Poems and Sonnets.* Urbana: University of Illinois Press, 1951.

Bate, Jonathan. *Shakespeare and the English Romantic Imagination.* Oxford: Clarendon Press, 1989.

———. *Shakespeare and Ovid.* Oxford: Oxford University Press, 1993.

Bates, Ronald. "Shakespeare's 'The Phoenix and Turtle.'" *Shakespeare Quarterly* 6 (1955): 19–30.

Baumlin, Tita French. "The Birth of the Bard: *Venus and Adonis* and Poetic Apotheosis." *Papers on Language and Literature* 26 (1990): 191–211.

Bermann, Sandra. *The Sonnet over Time: A Study in the Sonnets of Petrarch, Shakespeare, and Baudelaire.* Chapel Hill: University of North Carolina Press, 1988.

Blackmur, R. P. "A Poetics of Infatuation." In *The Riddle of Shakespeare's Sonnets.* New York: Basic Books, 1962.

Booth, Stephen. *An Essay on Shakespeare's Sonnets.* New Haven, CT: Yale University Press, 1969.

———, ed. *Shakespeare's Sonnets.* New Haven, CT: Yale University Press, 1977.

Brower, Reuben, Helen Vendler, and John Hollander, eds. *I. A. Richards: Essays in His Honor.* Oxford: Oxford University Press, 1973.

Colie, Rosalie. *Shakespeare's Living Art.* Princeton, NJ: Princeton University Press, 1974.

Copland, Murray. "The Dead Phoenix." *Essays in Criticism* 15 (1965): 279–287.

Cruttwell, Patrick. "A Reading of the Sonnets." *Hudson Review* 5 (1953): 554–570.

De Grazia, Margreta. "Babbling Will in Shakespeare's Sonnets 127 to 154." In *Spenser Studies: A Renaissance Poetry Annual I.* Pittsburgh: University of Pittsburgh Press, 1980.

Dubrow, Heather. *Captive Victors: Shakespeare's Narrative Poems and Sonnets.* Ithaca, NY: Cornell University Press, 1987.

———. "A Mirror for Complaints: Shakespeare's *Lucrece* and Genetic Tradition." In *Renaissance Genres: Essays on Theory, History, and Interpretation.* Cambridge, MA: Harvard University Press, 1986.

Empson, William. *Seven Types of Ambiguity.* London: New Directions, 1930.

———. *Some Versions of Pastoral.* Norfolk, CT: New Directions, 1935.

Feinberg, Nona. "Thematic of Value in *Venus and Adonis.*" *Criticism* 31 (1989): 21–32.

Felperin, Howard. "The Dark Lady Identified, or What Deconstruction Can Do for Shakespeare's *Sonnets.*" In *Shakespeare and Deconstruction.* New York: Peter Lang, 1988.

———. "Toward a Poststructuralist Practice: A Reading of Shakespeare's Sonnets. In *Beyond Deconstruction*. Oxford: Clarendon Press, 1985.

Fineman, Joel. *Shakespeare's Perjured Eye*. Berkeley: University of California Press, 1986.

———. *The Subjectivity Effect in Western Literary Tradition*. Cambridge, MA: The MIT Press, 1991.

Frye, Northrop. "How True a Twain." In *The Riddle of Shakespeare's Sonnets*. New York: Basic Books, 1962.

Garber, Marjorie. "Two Birds with One Stone: Lapidary Reinscription in The Phoenix and Turtle." *Upstart Crow* 5 (1984): 5–19.

Green, Martin. *The Labyrinth of Shakespeare's Sonnets*. London: Charles Skilton, Ltd., 1974.

Greene, Thomas M. "Anti-hermeneutics: The Case of Shakespeare's Sonnet 129." In *Poetic Traditions of the English Renaissance*. New Haven, CT: Yale University Press, 1982.

Herrnstein, Barbara, ed. *Discussions of Shakespeare's Sonnets*. Boston: Heath, 1964.

Hubler, Edward. *The Sense of Shakespeare's Sonnets*. Princeton, N.J.: Princeton University Press, 1952.

Hynes, Sam. "The Rape of Tarquin." *Shakespeare Quarterly* 10 (1959): 451–453.

Kerrigan, John, ed. *The Sonnets and the Lover's Complaint*. New York: Penguin, 1986.

Klause, John. "*Venus and Adonis:* Can We Forgive Them?" *Studies in Philology* 85 (1988): 353–377.

Knight, G.Wilson. *The Mutual Flame*. London: Methuen & Co. Ltd., 1955.

Krieger, Murray. *A Window to Criticism: Shakespeare's Sonnets and Modern Poetics*. Princeton, NJ: Princeton University Press, 1964.

Landry, Hilton. *Interpretations in Shakespeare's Sonnets*. Berkeley: University of California Press, 1963.

———, ed. *New Essays on Shakespeare's Sonnets*. New York: AMS Press, Inc., 1976.

Lanham, Richard. *The Motives of Eloquence: Literary Rhetoric in the Renaissance*. New Haven, CT: Yale University Press, 1976.

Leech, Clifford. "Venus and Her Nun: Portraits of Women in Love by Shakespeare and Marlowe." *Studies in English Literature 1500–1900* 5 (1965): 247–268.

Leishman, J. B. *Themes and Variations in Shakespeare's Sonnets*. New York: Harper & Row, 1966.

Lever, J. W. *The Elizabethan Love Sonnet*. London: Methuen, 1966.

Lindheim, Nancy. "The Shakesperean *Venus and Adonis.*" *Shakespeare Quarterly* 37 (1986): 190–203.

Mack, Maynard, and George deForest Lord, eds. *Poetic Traditions of the English Renaissance*. New Haven CT: Yale University Press, 1982.

Martin, Philip J. *Shakespeare's Sonnets: Self, Love and Art.* Cambridge: Cambridge University Press, 1972.

Maus, Katharine Eisaman. "Taking Tropes Seriously: Language and Violence in Shakespeare's *The Rape of Lucrece.*" *Shakespeare Quarterly* 37 (1986): 66–82.

Melchiori, Giorgio. *Shakespeare's Dramatic Meditations: An Experiment in Criticism.* Oxford: Clarendon Press, 1976.

Nejgebauer, A. "The Sonnets." *Shakespeare Survey* 15 (1962): 10–61.

Nelson, Lowry, Jr. "The Matter of Rime : Sonnets of Sidney, Daniel, and Shakespeare." In *Poetic Tradition of the English Renaissance.* New Haven, CT: Yale University Press, 1982.

Pequigney, Joseph. *Such Is My Love: A Study of Shakespeare's Sonnets.* Chicago: University of Chicago Press, 1985.

Prince, F. T. *The Poems: The Arden Edition of the Works of William Shakespeare.* London: Methuen, 1960.

Putney, Rufus. "*Venus and Adonis:* Amour with Humour." *Philological Quarterly* 20 (1974): 533–548.

Ramsey, Paul. "The Fickle Glass: A Study of Shakespeare's Sonnets." A*MS Studies in the Renaissance* 4 (1979).

Ransom, John Crowe. "Shakespeare at Sonnets." *Southern Review 3* (1938): 531–553.

Sedgwick, Eve. *Between Men: English Literature and Male Homosocial Desire.* New York: Columbia University Press, 1985.

Vendler, Helen. *The Art of Shakespeare's Sonnets.* Cambridge, MA: Harvard University Press, 1997.

Wilde, Oscar. "The Portrait of Mr. W. H." In *The Artist as Critic.* Chicago: University of Chicago Press, 1968.

Wilson, Rowden. "Shakespearean Narrative: *The Rape of Lucrece* Reconsidered." *Studies in English Literature 1500–1900* 28 (1988): 39–59.

Winny, James. *The Master-Mistress: A Study of Shakespeare's Sonnets.* London: Chatto & Windus, 1968.

Index of
Themes and Ideas

ALL'S WELL THAT ENDS WELL, 10

ANTONY AND CLEOPATRA, 75–76

AS YOU LIKE IT, 14

COMEDY OF ERRORS, 36

CYMBELINE, 76

HAMLET, 14, 53, 68, 81, 87

HENRY III, 76

HENRY IV PLAYS, 9, 13, 74, 75

LOVER'S COMPLAINT, THE, 75

LOVE'S LABOUR'S LOST, 9

LOVE'S MARTYR, 74, 77

MEASURE FOR MEASURE, 10, 11, 68

MIDSUMMER NIGHT'S DREAM, A, 74, 97

OTHELLO, 10, 53

"PHOENIX AND TURTLE, THE": aesthetic strength of, 52; "bird of loudest lay" in, 73–74; birds' respective genders in, 74–76; critical views on, 72, 73–78; Donne and, 77; as gentle, 12; ideal love in, 72, 76–78; past critical errors in analyzing, 73–74; phoenix in, 72, 73, 74–76; Platonism and, 76–78; sections of, 72, 73; summary analysis of, 72; turtledove in, 72, 74, 76

RAPE OF LUCRECE, THE: anaphora in, 83, 84; Brutus in, 81, 86–87; classical influences on, 79; closure and, 87–88; Collatine in, 79, 81, 83, 85, 86, 89; as complaint genre, 79; conclusion of, 87; critical views on, 81–89; as error-free, 14; greed in, 79; Hecuba's grief and, 81, 86; imagery in, 81; importance of language over passion in, 82–84; irony in, 88; language and accountability in, 84–86; Lucrece in, 79, 80–84, 85–86, 87, 88, 89, 93; moral and emotional reactions to personages in, 86–89; moral decisions and, 87; narrator in, 79, 81; Ovid and, 36, 79, 93, 94; publication of, 14; rhetorical ambiguities in, 86–89; rhetoric of desire in, 93–94; rhyme in, 79; self-revelation in, 82–83; Sonnet 129 and, 68; "stain" in, 89; summary analysis of, 79–81; Tarquin in, 79–80, 81, 82, 83, 84–85, 86, 88–89, 93–94; as tragedy, 81, 93; turtledove in, 74; *Venus and Adonis* and, 79, 82, 86, 87, 88, 93–94

RICHARD III, 75

ROMEO AND JULIET, 71, 74

SHAKESPEARE, WILLIAM: biography of, 13–14; misprision and, 35–36; sexuality and, 10

SONNET 1, 20

SONNET 2, 23

SONNET 5, 23

SONNET 10, 20

SONNET 11, 20

SONNET 14, 20

SONNET 15, 20

SONNET 16, 20, 22

SONNET 17, 20, 22

SONNET 19: beauty of youth in, 20–23; critical views on, 19–24; ideal love in, 15–16, 19–20; irony in, 10; opening of, 10; phoenix in, 15; time in, 15–16, 19–21, 23–24

SONNET 20, 20–21, 24, 30, 41, 49

SONNET 29, 35

SONNET 48, 26

SONNET 49, 26

SONNET 52, 26, 35, 41

SONNET 53: beauty in, 16, 26; critical views on, 25–33; friend as both one and many in, 27–28; imitation in, 32–33; innovations in, 32–33; irony in, 11; love in, 30–31; *one* and *every* in, 29; opening of, 11; paradox in, 28–30; Platonism and, 16, 25–27, 30–31; sexuality in, 30–31; *shade* and *shadow* in, 28–30; substance and shadows in, 16, 25–26, 27, 30

SONNET 54, 26

SONNET 55: classical roots of, 16, 35–36, 37–38; critical views on, 33–38; Homer and, 37; Horace and, 16, 35, 36; Ovid and, 35, 36; Petrarch and, 38; Pindar and, 37; Plautus and, 36; poetry as key to immortality and, 16, 33; power of poetry in, 16, 33–34; rhetorical strategy in, 35–37; rhyme in, 34–45, 60; Seneca and, 36; Virgil and, 37, 38

SONNET 56, 26

SONNET 57, 26, 38

SONNET 58, 26

SONNET 66, 55

SONNET 67, 27

SONNET 68, 27

SONNET 74, 56

SONNET 87: blame in, 43–44; critical views on, 39–41; disillusionment with love in, 17, 39–41, 43–44; irony in, 43, 44; "misprision" in, 42, 44–45; physical passion in, 41–42; poet's punctured dream in, 39–41; reading beyond text of, 42–43; whims of beloved in, 42–43

SONNET 93, 55

SONNET 94: ambivalences in, 52–54; critical views on, 45–55; flattery in, 45–47; flower in, 48, 54–55; as forerunner to Shakespeare's tragedies, 52–54; imagery in, 47–48; irony in, 47–48; morality in, 17, 54–55; plant metaphors in, 48, 54–55; readers' expectations and, 49–51, 53; sexuality in, 17; youth's inability to produce love in, 49

SONNET 95, 55

SONNET 106, 27

SONNET 113, 27

SONNET 114, 40

SONNET 115, 57, 58, 62

SONNET 116: critical views on, 55–64; immortality and, 55–57; negative assertions in, 59; poet's love for youth versus lust for mistress in, 61–62; refutation in, 62–64; reinscription in, 63, 64; rhetoric in, 57–58; rhyme in, 34–35, 60–61; sexuality in, 61–62; as single-minded and heterogeneous, 59; substance and emptiness in, 55–60; tone of, 55; true love in, 17–18, 56–58, 61–62

SONNET 124, 55, 56

SONNET 127, 10

SONNET 128, 62

SONNET 129: comparisons with, 68; critical views on, 65–71; "dark lady" in, 62, 70–71; epithets in, 67; evolution of emotion in, 65–67; "experience of spirit" and social class in, 69–70, 71; irony in, 68; late Shakespeare and, 11–12; paradox of praise in, 70–71; sexuality in, 18, 62, 65, 70; tone of, 55

SONNETS: aesthetic strength of, 52; analysis of, 15–18; conflicting urges within self in, 15; "dark lady" in, 15; "fair youth" in, 15, 21–23, 70, 71, 98; husbandry in, 69–70; ideal love in, 15–16; irony in, 9–12; narrators of, 9; poetry and progeny in, 21–23; publication of, 14, 15; rhyme in, 15; series of analogies in, 69; sexuality in, 10; *Venus and Adonis* and, 98

TEMPEST, THE, 76

TIMON OF ATHENS, 10

TITUS AND ANDRONICUS, 36

TROILUS AND CRESSIDA, 10, 74

TWO NOBLE KINSMEN, THE, 10

VENUS AND ADONIS: Adonis in, 31, 90–92, 93, 94–96, 97–98, 99, 100–102, 103, 104; beauty in, 16; as comedy, 81, 93, 94, 96, 97, 102–4; critical views on, 93–104; elegy and, 97; as error-free, 14; horses in, 98; love as heartbreaking in, 92; moral and emotional reactions to personages in, 86; mutability in, 98; narrator's detachment in, 92, 94–96; Ovid and, 36, 90, 93, 96, 97, 99, 102–4; publication of, 14; *The Rape of Lucrece* and, 79, 82, 86, 87, 88, 93–94; redemption in, 100–102; responses to characters in, 99–100; rhetoric of desire in, 90–91, 93–94, 103–4; rhyme in, 90; Sonnets and, 98; summary analysis of, 90–92; sympathy for characters in, 99–102; time and, 97; tone of, 93, 96; turtledove in, 74, 75; vegetative myth in, 97–98; Venus in, 90–92, 93, 94–96, 97–98, 99, 100–104; vulnerability and powerlessness in, 91, 96–98; Wat (hare) in, 91, 98